The Fifth Wheel Bible

-

Everything You Ever Wanted to Know About Fifth Wheel Trailers

-

by
Jerry Brown

Copyright © 2007 by Jerry Brown

All rights reserved. No part of this book shall be reproduced or transmitted in any form or by any means, electronic, mechanical, magnetic, photographic including photocopying, recording or by any information storage and retrieval system, without prior written permission of the publisher. No patent liability is assumed with respect to the use of the information contained herein. Although every precaution has been taken in the preparation of this book, the publisher and author assume no responsibility for errors or omissions. Neither is any liability assumed for damages resulting from the use of the information contained herein.

Unless otherwise noted, all photographs are by the author.

A few sections in the later chapters of this book were adapted from articles written by the author that were originally published online at NewRVer.com.

ISBN 978-0-7414-3839-3

Published by:

West Conshohocken, PA 19428-2713
Info@buybooksontheweb.com
www.buybooksontheweb.com
Toll-free (877) BUY BOOK
Local Phone (610) 941-9999
Fax (610) 941-9959

Printed in the United States of America

Published November 2012

Acknowledgments

I am indebted to Chuck Woodbury at RVTravel.com for opening the doors of opportunity to a previously unpublished but enthusiastic RV writer. After years of writing technical matter and corporate copy, I had only my online journal "Travels with Timmy" to submit to Chuck as a sample of the kind of writing that I hoped he was looking for. Besides publishing my articles and columns on his websites and newsletter, Chuck planted the seed that has germinated into this book.

Thanks go to Mike Mitchell of Nu-Wa Industries for sharing with me the early history of the fifth wheel trailer hitch and industry.

A round of thanks also goes out to all those folks who contribute their time and thoughtful suggestions at the various online forums. They helped me immensely and inevitably some of what I learned there has made its way into this volume.

I'm grateful to Liz Mares for reading my initial drafts and for her constructive comments and ideas. And I am especially thankful for the times we shared.

Finally, thanks to lifelong friends Tim and Mac Flood for their suggestions and for proofing the final draft.

Contents

Chapter 1 – Introduction

As you might surmise from the title, this book is intended to be a compendium about fifth wheel trailers. You'll find many books about the various aspects of recreational vehicles (RVs) in general. Other books cover the topic of trailers as a class of RVs; these usually include both fifth wheel and travel trailers, plus pop-ups, tent campers and just about anything that can be hitched. However, fifth wheel trailers are distinctly different from all of the other "towables." If you want to learn what there is to know about them, you've come to the right place.

We'll provide a lot of basic information, so if you are new to the subject, you should learn everything you might need to know, whether you are just curious, still evaluating various RV options, getting ready to buy, or even as a new owner wanting to learn as much as you can before heading out on your first adventure. We'd also like to provide useful information for more experienced RVers or fifth wheel owners. There's a lot to know and we hope you'll learn a few things that will make your fifth wheel experience easier and more enjoyable.

This is the book that I wish I'd had when I set out on my own RV adventure three years ago. I read a few books on general RVing, and they helped me with some basic information. But it wasn't until I got out and talked to people and then spent considerable time online reading many posts on a variety of forums that things started to come together for me. I'll share what I learned as I went through the process of deciding what type RV to buy and then selecting the fifth wheel that has worked out so well.

When I finally ventured out on the road in December 2004, I still had much learn. I hope that this book will help you to avoid some of the problems I had. Experience may be the best teacher, but perhaps you can profit from some of the things that I learned the hard way.

A short note on semantics: The term *fifth wheel trailer* is frequently shortened to just *fifth wheel* and the slang term *fiver* is also in common use. It is often written as *5er*, especially in online venues such as blogs and forums. For our purposes, we'll use fifth wheel and fiver interchangeably throughout this book.

Where did the term *fifth wheel* come from? We'll cover that topic in the next chapter, along with some history and background on what actually is a fiver. Moving along, we'll look at the advantages of fifth wheels as compared to motor homes and to travel trailers. Then we'll explore the fifth wheel universe, where there are now literally thousands of models to choose from. We'll provide some structure and suggest some strategies that should help you find the right trailer for your needs and budget. Then we'll delve into the subject of tow vehicles, essential information for prospective fifth wheelers. And no review of fifth wheels would be complete without a detailed review of the hitch that sets them apart from all other towable RVs.

If you already own a fiver, tow vehicle, and hitch, I think you'll find Chapter 2 interesting, but you may wish to skim Chapters 3 through 7 or skip forward to Chapter 8. Starting there, the last half of the book will be devoted to more operational topics, the "nuts and bolts" of tools and accessories, driving, towing, backing, parking, and other subjects related to enjoying and getting the most out of your fiver. Then we'll have a little fun going off the beaten track with our trailers. Finally, we'll provide some checklists to help you remember essential steps involved in departure and arrival sequences. Here and there you'll find tips that we have learned on our own or picked up along the way.

Please note: This book is not intended to replace your owner's manuals. You need to be familiar with details and operational procedures specific to your particular brand or model of trailer, hitch or other accessory. Only an owner's manual can provide this information. It's unlikely, but if anything in this book conflicts with your owner's manual, be sure to follow the manual. Hopefully this book presents details and fleshes out procedures in a way that complements those which manufacturers provide.

RVing is a wonderful way to experience this wonderful land of ours. I hope this book helps you to get out and enjoy all there is to see and do in a way that is uniquely yours. Happy Trails to you.

RVIA stock photo

Chapter 2 - What's a Fifth Wheel and How Did They Come About?

If we define *RVs* as self-contained, mobile living units, they've been around in one form or another even longer than the automobile. Of course they were known by other names in earlier times. The first camping trailers, called caravans, date back to late 19th century England. Covered wagons were even earlier and gypsy wagons go back hundreds of years. Motor homes first appeared early in the 20th century, along with many varieties of popup, tent and travel trailer. These were hugely popular in the 1920's and 1930's. But fifth wheels as we know them arrived on the scene much later, about the same time that Neil Armstrong was stepping out onto the moon.

Even before you picked up this book, you probably knew what fifth wheel trailers were, but did you know why they are called that? I've always been curious about the term *fifth wheel* myself. Does that refer to the trailer being supported at the front end by a tow vehicle acting as a sort of giant front wheel?

The Fifth Wheel Hitch

Actually, the term refers to the hitch and dates from the early days of the automotive industry, when it was first used on trucks. Early truck hitches consisted of some variation on a pin on the trailer that dropped into a receiver on the truck or tractor. The problem was that it took three people to complete a simple hitching operation – two to jack up and lower the trailer plus a driver to position the truck beneath. The horizontal, locking-jaw fifth wheel hitch was devised and patented in 1919. Now a singe person working alone, the truck driver, could couple and uncouple a trailer.

Why *fifth wheel*? The hitch is essentially a circular plate and the "kingpin" rotates in the center like an axle, so it resembles a wheel even though it is mounted horizontally over the rear truck axles. The name stuck and has been used in trucking ever since. The hitch itself has changed little over the years. However, the fifth wheel hitch now used in the RV world wasn't developed for another 50 years, until the late 1960's.

The First Fifth Wheel Trailers

At almost the same time that the fifth wheel hitch was being developed, outdoorsman and famed aviation pioneer Glenn H. Curtiss was working on improvements to early trailer designs. His first, called the "Motor Bungalow," was initially produced in 1919 by his half brother, Carl Adams, at the Adams Trailer Corp. Curtiss devised his own variation on

The 1919 Curtiss Motor Bungalow, complete with "pop-out" sides. Courtesy www.glennhcurtiss.com.

the fifth wheel hitch, an actual wheel and tire mounted horizontally over the rear axle of the tow car using four clamps in a square frame. The pin on the trailer was locked into the hub of the wheel. The inflated tire helped to dampen road vibrations and shocks, improving the ride and reducing wear and tear on the trailer. Only a few units of this first "fifth wheel trailer" were produced and the Motor Bungalow was discontinued in 1922.

Curtiss returned to the trailer world in 1928 with a lighter, more elegant design that he called the Aerocar Land Yacht.

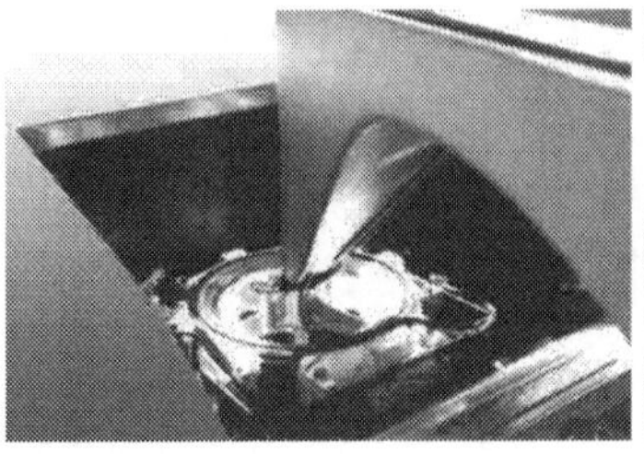

The Curtiss "Fifth Wheel" hitch and a restored 1936 Curtiss Aerocar. Courtesy Hindley's Garage.

It included lavish interiors and a padded artificial leather exterior, along with several "high tech" options. This expensive trailer was produced until 1940, still using the Curtiss hitch. Its departure from the scene marked the beginning of a 30 year hiatus in fifth wheel trailer design and production.

The Modern Fifth Wheel Era Begins

We pick up our story again in 1968, when the Classic Hitch Company of Sturgis, Michigan, designed and patented the first hitch created specifically for RVs. It was based on the tried and true fifth wheel concept employed by the trucking industry.

A modern fifth wheel trailer hitch

Their first design used a one inch diameter king pin, rather wimpy compared to the two inch pin that soon followed and remains in use today. Classic faced a chicken and egg situation though – they had a hitch but no market. The history gets a little muddled here, but they either helped local company Good Manufacturing to get started in the fifth wheel trailer business, or they convinced them to get into it. Either way, by 1969 Good had produced the Mayfair, the first modern fifth wheel trailer.

1970 NuWa HitchHiker, 27 foot fifth wheel. Courtesy NuWa Industries

Maybe it was a case of "if you build it, they will come." Within a year there were three more fifth wheels on the market: the Hylander from Osceola, Iowa, the WheelCamper, also from Michigan, and the HitchHiker from NuWa (pronounced "new way") Industries of Chanute, Kansas. Those early designs were all recognizable as fifth wheels because of the raised front section that still characterizes fifth wheel trailers today. But they were a little more like truck campers or Class C motor homes with a "crawl in" forward bedroom. Raised rooflines and lowered bedroom floors came a little later, evolving over time into today's split level floor plans.

The fiver concept caught on and by 1972 many of the major RV and trailer manufacturers had joined the fifth wheel game, including such household names as Winnebago and

A '70s era Terry Taurus, tiny but still in use. Note travel trailer "landing gear."

Airstream. Increased competition drove advancement in designs and also tended to weed out some of the players. Of the four original fifth wheel manufacturers, only NuWa survives today, in part by being one of the major innovators. Some of their early introductions include the first slide out (or glide room) in 1974 and the "stand up dressing area" -- the first effort to accommodate more height in the bedroom and bath area. They have also been an industry leader in floor plan design for many years.

Over the ensuing 35 years, fifth wheel trailers have continued to grow in size, comfort and popularity. As of 2006, over 22% of all RVs sold were fivers.

What is a Fifth Wheel?

That brings us up to date, but have we really answered the original question: "What is a fifth wheel?" The primary differentiator between a standard travel trailer and a fifth wheel is of course the hitch and the requirement that the tow

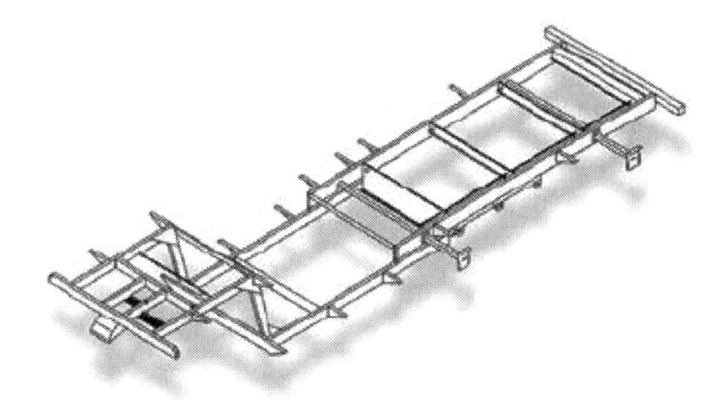

A typical fifth wheel frame. Note the pin box under the raised section.

vehicle must be some sort of truck capable of bearing it. Because the hitch is mounted in the truck bed, the trailer must have a raised front section such that it clears the back of the truck and provides attachment for the pin box. This is evident in the design of the fifth wheel frame, the example shown here being typical. That basic frame now supports a bewildering array of floor plans and options across the industry. We'll look at some of them in Chapter 4.

Alternative floor plans with the kitchen or living room in the front raised section were introduced early on, but the front bedroom layout prevailed and is now the industry standard. Most modern designs also include a sloping roofline, which gives the fifth wheel trailer the most spacious feel of any RV because of the added headroom in the main living sections.

The cutaway drawing in the accompanying illustration shows some typical fifth wheel construction details, including aluminum framing, wooden roof trusses – although many trailers now use aluminum roof trusses – and laminated exterior sidewalls. The drawing shows another feature unique to fivers: the two front legs, also known as landing gear, that support the trailer when unhitched and which are used to raise and lower it for leveling and coupling or uncoupling.

Typical fifth wheel trailer construction details.

Recent Fifth Wheel Developments

Don't get the idea that innovation in fifth wheel engineering is stagnant. The "toy hauler" concept is one fairly recent development. The popularity of so called Sport Utility trailers that are designed to carry ATVs and motorcycles is growing rapidly, particularly among younger buyers and families. Many manufacturers have added one or more models to their lineups.

The toy hauler "portable garage." RVIA stock photo.

When these rigs are camped and not "hauling toys," the back end is converted into living space. Some units have bedroom or dining room sections that are raised to accommodate the toys and lowered at camp.

Another fiver modification extends the front of the trailer forward over the cab of the tow vehicle. This concept was developed by Canadian manufacturer Glendale RV for their Titanium line. They state that it reduces wind drag, contributes to significant fuel savings, and provides

The aerodynamic "cab over" Titanium.

exceptional road handling and stability. By shifting the living area forward, the design also results in a shorter combined wheelbase versus the standard fiver of equivalent length.

And the slideout expansions continue. In 2002 Carriage, Inc., introduced the first five slide fifth wheel in its Carri-Lite line: three on the main level and two forward. The second slide in the bath/bedroom area provides for a very spacious master bedroom suite. Other five-slide configurations have followed, with four on the main level and one bedroom. Can full-side slides, which have been introduced on large Class A motor homes, be far behind?

Chapter 3 – Why Buy a Fifth Wheel?

If you happen to be a happy fifth wheel owner or if you've already decided that a fiver is right for you, then you may want to skip this chapter. Otherwise, read on, because we're going to talk about the advantages that fifth wheel trailers have over other RVs.

We'll need to break this subject into a couple of sections, since we'll be comparing fivers to both motor homes and to travel trailers, and there isn't much overlap in these discussions.

Fivers versus Motor Homes

Motor homes are divided into three classes: A, B and C. In general terms, Class A's are the largest and are typically built on a chassis that is specifically designed for the purpose. They are also usually the most well equipped and most expensive of the three classes. Class B's are essentially van conversions and are the smallest. Class C's are built on a truck chassis that includes the cab. All are self-contained.

Fifth wheels have two advantages over motor homes, regardless of Class. First, the unit can be parked and after unhitching, the tow vehicle is available for shopping, exploring or any other driving need. It's not necessary to pack things up every time you want to go somewhere. Travel trailers of course also share this advantage. Many motor home owners counter this advantage by towing a "dinghy," a car, small pickup or even SUV that they can use when their rig is parked. This obviously adds to the expense of owning and driving the combination. Also in this regard, don't forget that when you are off the road, the motor home will sit parked in the drive or storage lot, while the pickup used with the fiver is available for hauling or just every day driving.

The other advantage of fivers is economic: You simply get more living space for less money with a fifth wheel. It stands to reason, since you are not paying for a motor and drive train. Further, there's no driving seat, console or dashboard taking up living area.

One further advantage of fivers: excluding Class B's, you can expect better mileage from your truck while towing than you are likely to get from a motor home, provided that the units are of comparable size and similarly equipped.

Fivers versus Travel Trailers

The comparison between fifth wheels and travel trailers is considerably different. For starters, travel trailer owners share with their fiver counterparts the advantage of using the tow vehicle when their unit is parked. The differences are mainly in spaciousness, storage capacity and ease of towing.

The "split level" floor plan of fifth wheel trailers with its higher ceiling in the bedroom area provides a greater sense of separation between the living and sleeping areas. In most modern fivers the ceiling slopes up from back to front, enhancing the sense of spaciousness. The raised floor up front also opens up extensive storage areas under the bedroom that have no counterpart in travel trailers. One example of this additional capacity is in the placement of propane tanks. On travel trailers these are carried externally on the tongue, while on all fifth wheels the propane tanks are housed inside a separate forward compartment.

The other major advantage of fivers is in tow-ability. Travel trailers are designed to use the standard, bumper-mounted ball hitch. On fifth wheels the placement of the hitch inside the bed and over the rear axle of the tow vehicle results in a superior towing experience. Sway is virtually eliminated and bucking is reduced. Equalizing hitches, also called load distributing hitches, used in conjunction with travel trailers improve their stability, but fifth wheels are still better in this regard. In addition the combined length of trailer plus tow vehicle is shorter with fivers. This can make parking and maneuvering in tight areas easier. As far as backing, travel trailers respond a little more quickly, but there's probably no significant advantage there. With practice you can learn to back up and maneuver either fiver or travel trailer.

Another factor favoring fifth wheels is the ease of hitching. With full visibility of the hitch and king pin from within the tow vehicle, one person can easily and quickly complete a hookup. An experienced travel trailer owner working alone can usually get their ball hitch fairly close to the trailer's socket, but it is rare that they don't have to get back in their tow vehicle and jockey it into final position to complete the hitch. A second person makes the operation a little easier in both cases, but with a fifth wheel, an exact alignment is not necessary. The V-shaped opening in the hitch plate will guide the king pin to the center of the hitch.

What's right for you?

There's no short or right answer to this question. But I think there are a couple of considerations that can help you with your decision. First, are you planning to be fulltime RVers or vacation/weekend campers? Fulltimers are generally happier with larger and more fully equipped units such as Class A or larger Class C motor homes or fifth wheel trailers. Second, will you be on the move a lot with overnight and short stops or will you tend toward extended stays allowing time for local sightseeing and exploration? If you will be on the go, you may be happier with a motor home; otherwise, you may find a trailer more suitable.

At the risk of over simplifying, the following graphic may help you to visualize these choices.

RV Lifestyle

Weekends/Vacations → Full time

Camping style: Short stops ↓ Long stays

Camping style	Weekends/Vacations	Full time
Short stops	Smaller motor home	Larger motor home
Long stays	Larger towable	Fifth wheel

My experience

In my case the decision was fairly easy. Economics and the ability to unhitch and drive a tow vehicle steered me away from motor homes. My desire to spend days or even weeks at a time camped at particular locations reinforced the choice. Then, as I looked at trailers, my plans for solar power pretty much sealed the deal for fifth wheels. There is simply no adequate storage area for a bank of deep cycle batteries on most travel trailers.

It has turned out to be the right decision. My fiver has allowed me to enjoy the RV lifestyle of my dreams.

Chapter 4 – Understanding the Fifth Wheel Universe

At the present time, there are some 140 RV manufacturers in the US and Canada. Of these, about 80 build fifth wheel trailers. While some of these companies build only one model, others offer as many as four or five. Typically each model is available in several floor plans and each of those may be offered in various sizes. The permutations can get a little overwhelming – the number of unique fifth wheel designs currently available probably numbers in the thousands. And then there are the options.

What we'd like to do in this chapter is provide an overview of the fifth wheel market and suggest some strategies for coping with the possibly bewildering spectrum of products and choices. Our ultimate goal is to help you, the buyer, find the trailer that's right for your budget, needs and style.

The Range in Fifth Wheel Trailers

A couple of photographs may give you some idea of the range in fivers that we are talking about. The first is the 19 foot Scamp, the smallest of all fifth wheel trailers. This single axle unit is light enough to be towed by a four-cylinder truck.

At the small end, the 19 foot Scamp. Courtesy Scamp Trailers

At the other end of the spectrum, a number of manufacturers build 40 foot trailers, some of them extending to as much as 44 feet in actual end-to-end length. These units all require triple axles to handle their weight. They may also call for a medium- or heavy-duty truck as a tow vehicle. The massive Weekend Warrior bunkhouse toy hauler shown is an example of fifth wheels in the largest sizes.

The 39 foot Weekend Warrior, an example of the largest fifth wheels.

While we're on the subject of size, there is one other variable – some manufactures build 102-inch-wide coaches, six inches more than the standard eight foot width. These units provide additional living room, but you should be aware that a few states have restrictions on wide body trailers. They can be towed on all Interstate highways, but travelers who plan to drive on US and state highways or secondary roads would be well advised to check traffic laws in their area.

Fiver Floor Plans

Let's turn now to floor plans. At any given size, the typical fifth wheel model will be available in several layouts. Builders like to designate them with numbers such as 27 RL, 295 FKTG,

37 CKRD, 34.5 QGRLR, and so on. Perhaps surprisingly, there is order in this alphabet soup. The numerical part is easy -- it's the nominal length in feet, although in practice the true front-to-bumper length may be up to 10% longer. And in general, most of the alphabetical number segments are decipherable. For example, the RL means Rear Lounge; you may also see RK for Rear Kitchen. Many of the longer designations can also be decoded, such as CKRD indicating Center Kitchen Rear Dining. Other examples: IK means Island Kitchen, UK is U-shaped Kitchen, and QG is Quad (i.e. four) Glide. There are many more possibilities. But don't get caught up in them; if the meaning is not fairly obvious, it may be more trouble than it's worth trying to figure it out.

Despite this apparent complexity, the floor plan situation is really pretty simple. For starters the master bedroom is always forward, with the bathroom usually just aft and the kitchen, dining and lounge (living room) areas on the main level. The two main alternatives are rear kitchen and rear lounge with lots of variations in the details. Almost all contemporary fivers have at least one slideout on the main level; as you move upscale, higher end models may have two or three plus one or two in the bedroom area.

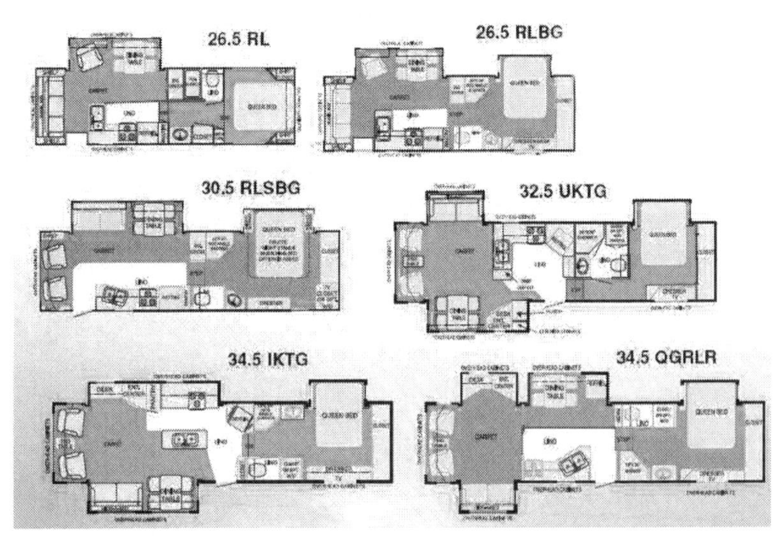

Partial floor plan listing for one fifth wheel line; all rear lounge configurations

Take a look at the floor plan illustration and notice the progression: We start with just a single slideout in the living area. Then a bedroom slide is added. Almost all larger fivers have a bedroom slideout, so they can offer walk around queen or king sized beds. The next model is four feet longer with more room in both the bedroom and main levels. Next a third slide is added and with an expanded U-shaped kitchen. The next model is a couple of feet larger with an island kitchen. Finally, we have a quad glide, with four slides. In this sequence we've gotten longer and added a lot of living space, but the basic configuration is still bedroom and bath forward and raised, kitchen center and lounge aft.

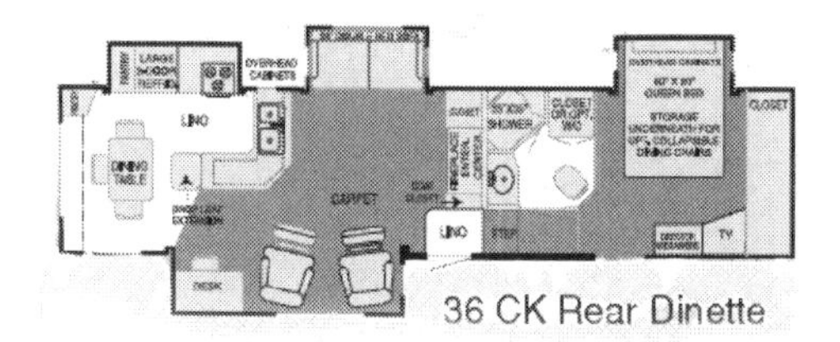

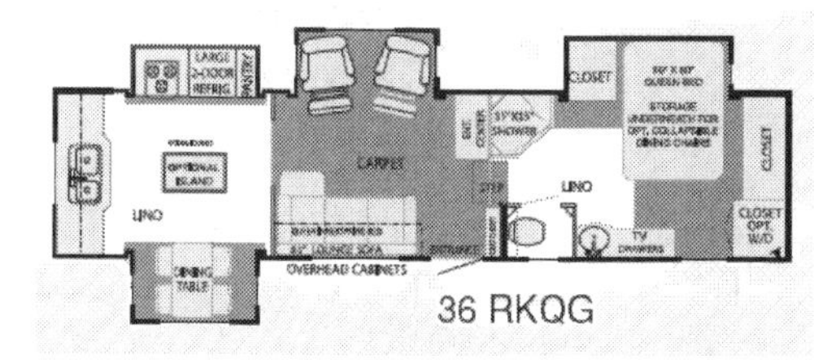

Another model in two rear kitchen floor plan configurations.

The other basic configuration is rear kitchen, with the lounge area central. You will see many variations on this arrangement; two are illustrated, both based on four slideouts.

A few models are available with a second bedroom or a "bunkhouse" in the rear, suitable for the sleeping needs of larger families.

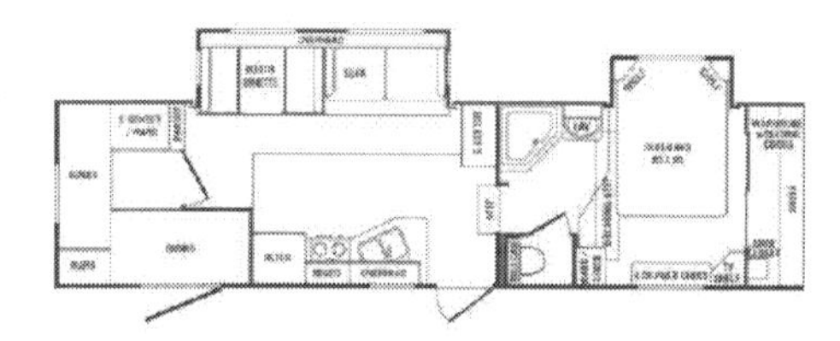

Bunkhouse configuration with center living area.

Finally there are the toy haulers, sometimes called sport

utility (SU) trailers. Since the primary function of the rear section in these is to carry ATVs, dirt bikes and the like to and from recreational sites, these units must have a large "garage" space available, six feet or more from the rear drop-down hatch or ramp. However, once at camp, this space can be used as additional living space. Furniture that was raised to make room for toys can be lowered, dining booths in some layouts, beds in others.

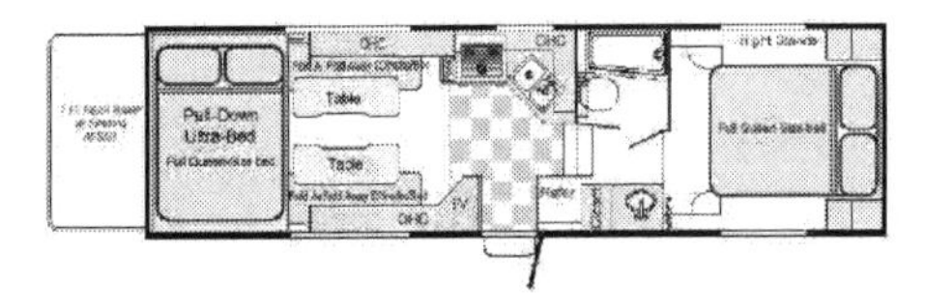

A sport utility or toy hauler model with queen bed that can be raised and lowered.

A Question of Value

Moving beyond floor plans, another variable in understanding the fifth wheel universe is value. The main reason that RV builders provide multiple model lines is so that they can offer a range of price points. That is, for a particular size or configuration, you will find that appliances, amenities, décor and overall quality of materials will vary as you move from less to more expensive models. Higher end models tend also to have more and larger glide rooms or slideouts, hence more living space for a given length. They may also be better insulated. Often lower end models are not designed and rated for full time living. In fact full time occupancy of such a trailer may invalidate the manufacturer's warranty

For the buyer working with a relatively fixed budget, the selection process may entail in part a tradeoff between size and spaciousness versus higher quality appliances and materials.

Capacity Considerations

Let's turn now to more mundane aspects of the fiver world: cargo carrying capacity and storage, including fresh and waste water tanks. We need to start this discussion with a couple of definitions. Every trailer has a Gross Vehicle Weight Rating (GVWR) and an Unloaded (or dry) Vehicle Weight (UVW). You will find the GVWR printed on the Federal Certification Tag on the outside of every new trailer. GVWR is the maximum weight that the vehicle is designed to carry, based on axle and tire size, brakes and other factors. UVW is the weight of the vehicle as it left the factory.

MANUFACTURED BY / FABRIQUE PAR: THOR INDUSTRIES/DUTCHMEN DATE: March 2004

GVWR/PNBV 4790 KG(10560 LB)

GAWR/PNBE	TIRES/PNEU	RIMS/JANTE	COLD INFL. PRESS./PRESS. DE GONFL. A FROID
FRONT/ 1996 KG AVANT (4400 LB)	ST225/75R15(D)	15X6	448 KPA SINGLE DUAL (65 PSI/LPC) [X] [ ]
INTERM/ KG INTERM (LB)			KPA SINGLE DUAL (PSI/LPC) [ ] [ ]
REAR/ 1996 KG ARRIERE (4400 LB)	ST225/75R15(D)	15X6	448 KPA SINGLE DUAL (65 PSI/LPC) [X] [ ]

Federal Certification Tag for my trailer

To determine the Cargo Carrying Capacity (CCC), which is basically the capacity to haul all of your "stuff," you start with the GVWR, subtract the UVW, then subtract the weight of water and propane that the vehicle carries, figuring 8.3 pounds per gallon for water and 4.2 for propane. You will find these figures printed on the RVIA Weight Label affixed to the inside of a cabinet somewhere in the trailer. In addition, they should be included with the owner's manual.

TRAILER WEIGHT INFORMATION

VIN OR SERIAL NUMBER 47CFCRP254P650886 27RL-M5

GVWR (GROSS VEHICLE WEIGHT RATING) IS THE MAXIMUM PERMISSIBLE WEIGHT OF THIS TRAILER WHEN FULLY LOADED. IT INCLUDES ALL WEIGHT AT THE TRAILER AXLE(S) AND TONGUE OR PIN.

UVW (UNLOADED VEHICLE WEIGHT) IS THE WEIGHT OF THIS TRAILER AS MANUFACTURED AT THE FACTORY. IT INCLUDES ALL WEIGHT AT THE TRAILER AXLE(S) AND TONGUE OR PIN. IF APPLICABLE, IT ALSO INCLUDES FULL GENERATOR FLUIDS, INCLUDING FUEL, ENGINE OIL, AND COOLANTS.

CCC (CARGO CARRYING CAPACITY) IS EQUAL TO GVWR MINUS EACH OF THE FOLLOWING, UVW, FULL FRESH (POTABLE) WATER WEIGHT (INCLUDING WATER HEATER), AND FULL LP-GAS WEIGHT.

CARGO CARRYING CAPACITY (CCC) COMPUTATION	POUNDS	KILOGRAMS
GVWR	10560	4790
MINUS UVW	8236	3736
MINUS FRESH WATER WEIGHT OF 52 GALLONS @8.3 LB/GAL	434	197
MINUS LP-GAS WEIGHT OF 14 GALLONS @4.2 LB/GAL	59	27
=CCC FOR THIS TRAILER*	1831	831

*DEALER INSTALLED EQUIPMENT WILL REDUCE CCC.
CONSULT OWNER MANUAL(S) FOR SPECIFIC WEIGHING INSTRUCTIONS AND TOWING GUIDELINES.
ALL WEIGHTS ARE APPROXIMATE

RVIA RVIA Weight Label from owner's manual

Here's an example based on my trailer:

GVWR		10,560 lbs
UVW		2,324 lbs
Gross Capacity		8,236 lbs
Fresh Water	8.3 x 52	434 lbs
Propane	4.2 x 14	59 lbs
CCC		1,831 lbs

So I can haul 1800 pounds of stuff: all of my dishes, food, clothes, books, tools, toys, etc. And where am I going to put all this stuff? That's the other part of cargo capacity. Fifth wheels usually have large storage areas forward under the master bedroom, but you also need good storage within for clothes, bedding, dishes, pots, pans, and everything else you want to have conveniently available.

Getting back to water, this is partly a question of what sort of camping you will be doing. If you will spend most of your time hooked up to water and sewage, then holding capacity won't matter as much. On the other hand, if you are planning to do a lot of dry camping, then fresh and waste water capacity should be a consideration in your selection process.

That completes our overview of the fiver landscape. If you are new to RVs and fifth wheels in particular, all of this information may seem a bit overwhelming. Our suggestion is to adopt a systematic approach. In the next chapter we'll share some ideas based on our experience.

Chapter 5 – The Right Fifth Wheel for You

Before you shop

We'll assume here that you have already analyzed the different types and classes of RVs and that you have decided that a fifth wheel best fits your needs. Your next step should be to determine what you can afford. This doesn't have to be exact, but knowing your budget is important in narrowing down the scope of what to look at. The question of new versus used plays into this. Obviously you will find more trailer for less money in the used market with the obvious tradeoffs – warranty, wear, potential mechanical problems, etc. It's the same situation as buying a used car, except perhaps more complicated in that there are more systems and more ways that the vehicle can sustain wear and tear. But it's still a bottom line question: what you can afford helps define what you should spend time looking at.

At this point we suggest that you go window shopping. Try to take in an RV show. These are held all across the country; to find a show near you visit the RV Industry Association web site at www.rvia.org. Dozens of manufacturers bring various RV models to these events. Don't go with the idea of buying; despite the hype, you can usually get the same deals that are offered at shows later on. Your goal at the show is to check out as many units in your general price range as you can. Look at different floor plans, examine materials and workmanship, ask questions. Take plenty of notes. What features do you like, what layouts appeal to you? Imagine living in each unit for days or weeks at a time. Check out bathroom arrangements, some can be pretty cozy. Pick up brochures for all of the models that you like.

Understand your needs

By now you should have a better idea of what's available and what appeals to you. Now it's time to take a look at your needs. Get out pencil and paper and take a mental tour of your ideal fifth wheel. Make notes on what you think you need.

Bedroom – Do you need the extra room a slide provides?
How much closet space?
Bath – Need a full size shower?
Kitchen – How much counter space, pantry, storage?
Dining arrangements – Booth or table and chairs?

And so on. Then try to estimate your cargo needs, considering both weight and storage space. Finally consider fresh and waste water capacity as discussed previously. You'll need more of both if you plan to do a lot of dry camping.

When I went through this exercise, I was single and working with a limited budget. So I figured I could do without the bedroom slide. But I was planning to work full time from the unit, so I needed an area that could accommodate a desk. Working from the dining table was not an option for me. Based on floor plans I had seen in the 25 – 30 foot range of trailers, I felt that the rear lounge layout would work best. I would plan to replace one of the lounge chairs with a desk, but I'd have to be sure that I could fit the desk in and still operate a slide, which I had decided I'd like in the kitchen/lounge area. I planned on extensive dry camping, so I added larger fresh and waste water storage to my list. I also planned to install a solar power setup, so I would need a good area for extra batteries. And I decided I wanted an all aluminum frame to eliminate the possibility of structural rot if my trailer should ever develop a hidden leak.

Now I was ready for serious shopping. I had a pretty clear visual picture of what I was looking for. Do your homework. You will find it makes locating the right trailer much less stressful.

Shop 'til you drop

There were probably a dozen RV dealerships within a hundred miles of my home. I visited most of them over the course of a couple of weekends. I probably walked through twice that many fivers with a rear lounge floor plan in the 27-30 foot range. I took notes on all and was able to weed out several as I went along. Then I sat down and carefully reviewed the ones I still liked, about a half dozen. I made up a chart listing specifics such as water storage capacity, cargo capacity, list price, and so on. I included notes on particular points I liked or disliked. I ranked the units on these details and found that two of them were quite close and scored better than the others. I also spent a little time online at a couple of RV forums checking for negative feedback on the models I liked. And I reviewed the RV Ratings CD Guide for Travel Trailers/Fifth Wheels which I had purchased from RV.org.

At the end of a process like this, you may determine that to meet your needs, you will need to order a new unit from the factory. In my case the two that I ranked highest were available on a dealer's lot, both at the same dealer in a nearby city. I went back and gave both a thorough going over. Then I asked the sales guy to let me have a little time to just sit in each unit to see how it felt. I think I could have been happy with either, but in the end, it came down to the shower. One unit had a small tub and shower cramped into a tiny bathroom with the toilet. The other had a full-sized shower and separate toilet closet. For full time living, I decided I wanted the roomy bathroom.

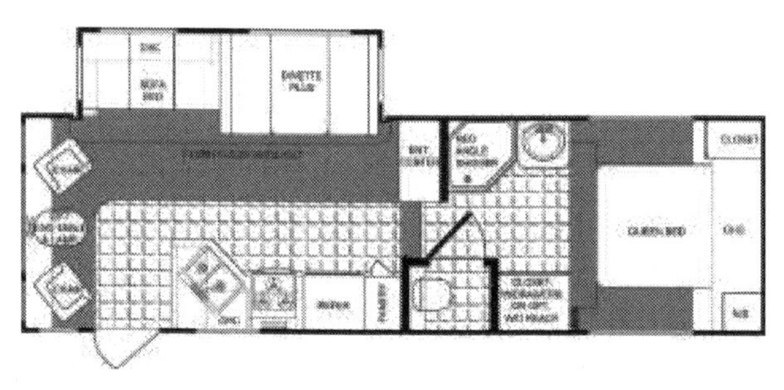

Floor plan of my fifth wheel

Cutting a deal

It was time to negotiate. There are other books available on negotiating techniques (one of which I had read), so I won't go into detail on that here. But I did prepare by determining the MSRP (Manufacturer's Suggested Retail Price) and making a list of things that I wanted included in the deal. These were 1) a hitch installed in my truck, 2) a slideout awning, 3) replace the dinette and chairs with a booth in matching décor, 4) extend the bed platform to accommodate a full-sized queen mattress, 5) replace the cheap short queen mattress with a full-sized one of better quality. I set a bottom line and mentally prepared myself to walk away if I didn't get it. I made my first offer at 2/3 of MSRP, to include the five items above. After some back and forth, we ended up at about 25% off MSRP with the first four items included. I thought it was a good deal. I later bought my own mattress and donated the cheapo to charity.

I hope this information helps you find the right fifth wheel for your unique needs and style. To sum up: learn all you can, understand what you really want, and have patience.

Good luck in cutting a deal. And while we're on the subject of working with a dealer, we have one more important topic.

The Pre-Delivery Inspection – Your chance to get it right

Before you drive your new fiver off the lot, you've got one more important task: the Pre-Delivery Inspection or PDI. Dealer service personnel will walk you through your unit and explain how things work. This is your chance to make sure that everything works and that you know how to work everything. As long as your unit is still on the dealer's lot, you are still in control. Take full advantage of this opportunity.

When you schedule your PDI with the dealer, try to make it early in the day so that you will have all the time you need.

Late afternoon PDIs can turn into rush jobs as closing time approaches. You will probably need at least two hours - the bigger the unit, the more time you need to allow.

Prepare for your PDI. Write down all of your questions and make a checklist of everything you want to cover. If possible obtain the user manuals and review them in advance. Note any areas that you aren't clear on. Bring a clipboard or notebook and be prepared to take lots of notes. Consider bringing a video camera or voice recorder to supplement your written notes.

During your PDI, try everything: open every window, door and drawer; test every light and electrical outlet; check the appliances and entertainment systems; run water in the sinks, shower and toilet; look for leaks. Your unit has both 120-volt AC and 12-volt DC (battery operated) fixtures and appliances. Make sure the refrigerator works in both electrical and LP modes; likewise the water heater. Test the sinks and shower on city water (hose attached) and with the onboard water pump. Is the pump noisy? Is the pressure adequate? Operate all slideouts. Take notes on anything that needs fixing or adjusting.

On the outside, check all the locks and latches. Go through the process of hooking up city water and shore power, as well as filling the fresh water tank. Make sure you know how to hook up the sewer hose and operate the gray and black water valves. This is one area where you won't be able to do a full operational test on the lot, but at least go through the motions. Learn how to operate the awnings. Look underneath the unit. Is anything loose? Are there any leaks? Go through the process of leveling the unit and crank down the stabilizer jacks. Review the hitching procedure and check that the hitch height is sufficient and the trailer is near level when hitched (see Chapter 7 for details).

Ask lots of questions. Refer to your written questions and checklist. Go over recommended maintenance schedules.

After you finish the PDI, review your list of issues with the service department. Make arrangements to have everything taken care of to your satisfaction. You can, of course, always get things fixed later on warranty, but it's a lot easier to get the dealer to agree to minor adjustments before you accept the unit and sign on the dotted line.

I've been very pleased with my fiver. As of this writing, I've lived in it nearly full time for two years. Even after PDI issues were taken care of I experienced a few miscellaneous problems early on, but I was able to have everything taken care of on warranty to my satisfaction.

Chapter 6 – Tow Vehicles for Fifth Wheels

With fifth wheel trailers there is one non-negotiable: If you are going to move it, you must have a truck. Travel trailers can be towed by cars, station wagons and SUVs, but only a truck is capable of towing a fiver for the simple reason that a truck bed is needed for mounting the fifth wheel hitch.

Truck classifications and ratings

Trucks are divided into light-duty, medium-duty, and heavy-duty classifications depending on hauling capacity, defined as gross vehicle weight rating (the same GVWR that we saw for trailer weight ratings). GVWR is the maximum load the vehicle is rated for, including fuel, passengers and any cargo, plus the weight of the payload, in our case the pin weight of the trailer (more on this shortly). The GVWR ratings for light, medium and heavy-duty classifications are as follows:

Class	GVWR	Examples
Light duty	Up to 14,000 lbs.	Most pickups and vans up to 1 ton
Medium duty	14,000 – 33,000 lbs.	Cargo and larger delivery trucks
Heavy duty	Over 33,000 lbs.	Big rig tractors, dump trucks

Pickup trucks, the most common fifth wheel tow vehicles, are all light duty trucks by this rating – even one ton models. You will see medium duty trucks towing many of the largest fifth wheels and heavy duty trucks used as tow vehicles are not uncommon. Although these larger trucks get lower fuel mileage, their increased towing capacity and braking capabilities, especially on grades, make them attractive tow vehicles.

Along with GVWR, trucks also are rated for the amount of weight they can safely tow. This Gross Combined Weight Rating (GCWR) includes the full loaded weight of both truck and trailer. Both the GVWR and GCWR are provided for all trucks by the manufacturers. You'll find them in the owner's manual and on a plate affixed to the driver side door. It is not safe to exceed either of these ratings.

MFD BY DAIMLERCHRYSLER CORPORATION DATE OF MFR 7-05 GVWR 4083 KG(09000 LB)

GAWR FRONT	WITH TIRES	RIMS AT	COLD
2359 KG(5200 LB)	LT265/70R17E	17X8.0	410 KPA(60 PSI)
GAWR REAR	WITH TIRES	RIMS AT	COLD
2727 KG(6010 LB)	LT265/70R17E	17X8.0	485 KPA(70 PSI)

Weight ratings for my Dodge 2500 pickup

We mentioned pin weight, the portion of the weight of the fifth wheel that will be carried by the tow vehicle. For purposes of estimating the GVWR of a tow vehicle, use 20% of the trailer's GVWR. This leads us to one additional rating: Gross Axle Weight Rating (GAWR). In the case of fifth wheels, most of the pin weight is transferred directly to the rear axle, so the rear GAWR may also be a concern. We'll illustrate these concepts by utilizing the ratings on my pickup and trailer. I drive a Dodge Ram 2500, four wheel drive, long bed, diesel and tow a Colorado 27RL. My ratings and weights are:

Trailer GVWR	10,560 lbs
Pin weight @20%	2,112 lbs
Truck GVWR	9,000 lbs
Truck GCWR	20,000 lbs
Rear GAWR	6,010 lbs
Truck "Curb" Weight	6,106 lbs
Truck with fuel & 2 passengers	6,700 lbs

So lets see...

Loaded truck plus trailer GVWR = 17,260 lbs, well under GCWR. Good.
Loaded truck plus pin weight = 8,812 lbs, under GVWR. Good.
Rear axle load, figure half of loaded truck plus pin weight = 5,462 lbs, under rear GAWR. Good.
We'll cover how you can determine your actual truck and trailer weights in Chapter 10.

I won't wade into the Dodge/Ford/Chevy discussion. All are good trucks and each has its adherents. The weight ratings for Ford 250s and Chevy/GMC 2500s similarly equipped are about the same as for my Dodge. Moving up to the 350/3500 models provides an incremental improvement in ratings. You have to jump into the medium duty range, the 450/4500 or 550/5500 models to substantially increase hauling and towing capabilities.

Dual wheels (duallys) are popular with many owners of larger fivers. However, I'm not sure they are worth the extra cost. In the first place, they only increase the GVWR and GCWR ratings by about 15%. On the other hand, the GAWR is improved substantially, on the order of 50%. So if your trailer has a very heavy pin weight, duallys might be a good choice.

However, there are disadvantages. Besides the obvious expense of two extra tires, your already large pickup will be about 18 inches wider, making it all the harder to park when you take it shopping without the trailer. I don't know how many dually equipped pickups I have seen with damaged fiberglass wheel well fender extensions. In addition, I have read that duallys are more likely to skid on snow or ice and they may be more prone to aqua-planing in heavy rain.

Gas or Diesel

This topic is sometimes controversial, with adherents on both sides of the issue. I've already stated that I drive a diesel, so you know where I stand. But I'll try to stick to the facts, present the advantages of both, and let you decide what's right for you.

I should clarify that I am not an expert when it comes to automotive power plants and transmissions. I can't talk torque and compare axle ratios. For our purposes here, we're going to assume engines of roughly equivalent power, which I believe to be the case when you compare typical stock models of either gas or diesel power in a particular class (say ¾ ton). Everything that I have been able to find on the subject points to the following: First, both will get you up a hill at about the same speed. Second, the diesel will get on the order of 20% more miles per gallon of fuel.

When diesel was cheaper than regular gasoline, always the case until recently, the better mileage of diesels made for a compelling economic case. If diesel remains priced the same as or more than premium gasoline, as it has been lately, that advantage is moot. From an environmental standpoint, diesel burns cleaner, and less fuel consumption means less carbon emission. As bio-diesel becomes more available, those of us driving diesels will have the opportunity to do a little more for the environment.

One other factor is worth mentioning here. In general, gasoline is more readily available than diesel. As a rough estimate, probably less than half of all gas stations sell diesel. If you happen to be on a long, lonesome stretch somewhere, or driving late at night, your odds of finding fuel when you need it are better if that fuel is gasoline.

Short bed or long?

Another consideration in selecting a tow vehicle for your fifth wheel trailer, assuming that you are going the pickup route, is the bed size. As in other factors, there are arguments in favor of each. If you already have a truck, you may wish to make do with it; otherwise, it pays to understand the options, think about what will best suit your needs, and then make your choice.

The main advantages of short bed trucks are evident when unhitched from the trailer: they are more maneuverable, easier to park, and, being somewhat lighter, will get better fuel mileage. The disadvantage is that you need a sliding hitch, an extended pin box (if available for your trailer), or both so as to avoid damage to the cab in tight turns. We'll discuss these hitches further in the next chapter. During normal operation, the sliding hitch is maintained in the forward position to keep the pin weight on or forward of the rear axle. But in that position there is inadequate clearance between trailer nose and truck cab for sharp turns. Thus you need to stop, release the slide, make the turn, and then reposition again for normal operation. Note: Highway driving with a sliding hitch in the rear position, behind the rear axle, is unsafe. It may affect steering and control of the pickup. An extended pin box on the trailer may also be required in order to ensure adequate clearance between trailer and truck cab.

The situation for long beds is just the reverse. Advantages of the long bed truck: the standard, non-sliding hitch is less expensive and the truck can haul longer loads easier than the short bed when used without the trailer.

Four-wheel drive

Probably the final decision to ponder in selecting a tow vehicle is whether to opt for four-wheel drive. It's expensive and adds weight, thereby adversely affecting mileage and possibly the GVWR of the truck. My advice: if you only drive paved roads and stop at commercial campgrounds or state and national parks, forget four-wheel. If, like me, you plan to get off the beaten path and into the back country, if you think you'll be doing any serious boondocking, then give four-wheel serious consideration. Here, by the way, I define boondocking as camping "in the boonies," not overnighting at Wally's or Home Depot. I have on many occasions been grateful that I had four-wheel drive out in the back country.

A final thought on this topic: four-wheel drive improves the resale value of a pickup, so you may recoup some of the extra cost over the long haul. And if the 4x shift lever on your truck ever saves you a tow, it may pay for itself right there.

Truck first or trailer?

So, should you start with a truck, then buy a trailer? Or vice versa? My advice: If you have a truck that you like and would like to keep, check out its weight ratings. This will tell you how much trailer you can tow with it. Then decide if a trailer in that weight range will fit your needs. Take a long term view on this -- you are likely to keep the trailer longer than the truck, so don't over value your current truck. Also, remember to consider bed size, fuel and four-wheel drive in this review.

However, if you have neither truck nor trailer, then by all means, select your trailer first; then size a truck to tow it. You're much more likely to arrive at an optimal truck-trailer combination.

Chapter 7 – The Fifth Wheel Hitch

So far we've covered trailer and truck - let's move on to the element that holds them together. As we noted earlier, the basic fifth wheel trucking hitch has been around for almost 90 years and the RV version is nearing 40. It's a safe, proven and easy to use device, provided that it is properly installed, maintained and used.

A fifth wheel trailer hitch consists of two main sections: a base and a rocking or dual-tilt skid plate assembly. The base is anchored to the truck's frame and provides a platform for the plate, which includes the locking mechanism. Typically the plate is mounted on the base so as to allow side-to-side rocking and the hitch plate itself pivots front-to-back. This dual-mode rocking motion is necessary to accommodate dips and uneven sections of road or driveway turns without damage to the hitch components. Inadequate freedom of movement can result in extra wear and tear as well as some possibly alarming noises.

The skid plate has a V-shaped cutout leading to the center pivot point. This makes hitching easier by guiding the king pin into the plate if it is not perfectly aligned. Once in place, the spring-loaded hitch jaws, slide-bar or hooking mechanism close, capturing the pin. There is also a handle for releasing the hitch and a locking catch that can prevent accidental or malicious release.

Hitch models and types

Several companies make fifth wheel hitches for the RV industry and they typically offer multiple models. All are safe and functional when used as intended and within the rated weight ranges. More expensive models offer additional features which may improve their functionality or ease of use. They usually include a longer warranty as well. It may be worth shopping around to understand what's available and at what cost.

My Reese 16K hitch

The two main types of fiver hitches are stationary and sliding. As we mentioned in Chapter 6, sliding hitches may be necessary with short bed trucks to ensure enough clearance between truck cab and trailer nose when making tight turns. During normal operation, the hitch is positioned over the rear axle to ensure safe and balanced towing. It can be moved to the rear when necessary. This is done by stopping, releasing the slide handle, and then slowly pulling the truck forward while the trailer brakes are held using the brake controller. The hitch should lock in at the rear position, making it safe to maneuver into camp sites or negotiate sharp turns. The procedure is reversed to return the hitch to the forward towing position. It is not safe to tow at normal speeds with a sliding hitch in the rear position. This places the pin weight behind the rear axle, which can cause steering problems or instability with the tow vehicle.

PullRite makes a "SuperGlide" sliding hitch that automatically adjusts the spacing between the trailer and the pickup cab during turns, without requiring the driver to exit the vehicle and manually operate the slide. A similar hitch is the Hijacker AutoSlide. These may be worth checking out if you have a short bed truck.

While we are on the subject of hitch types, from time to time you may also see fifth wheel trailers in tow using something called a "gooseneck" hitch. This hitch is based on a ball-type hitch mounted in the bed of the tow vehicle. It's sort of a cross between fifth wheel and traditional bumper-mounted ball hitches. Adapters are available for matching a fifth wheel pin box to the gooseneck ball. Large utility trailers commonly utilize the gooseneck hitch, and if their owners also tow a fiver, they often find it convenient to use the same hitch.

Hitch sizing, installation and maintenance

Just as with the fiver and tow vehicle, fifth wheel hitches have weight ratings, and they are just as important. Towing a trailer with an undersized hitch is unsafe, risking separation. The last thing you want to see is your trailer veering off in a different direction from your truck. As you would expect, the Max Gross Trailer Weight is the most total weight of trailer that the hitch is rated for. The other rating is Max King Pin Weight. The numbers on my Reese 16K hitch are 16,000 and 4,000 pounds respectively, both well over the corresponding weights for my trailer.

The installation of most current fifth wheel hitch designs is generally consistent from brand to brand and model to model. A pair of bed rails sits on the floor of the truck or pickup and is bolted through to the frame via a set of heavy duty mounting brackets. Some brands include fully removable rails using mounting posts in place of bolts. The base of the hitch is then attached to the bed rails using heavy grooved pull pins secured with hitch or spring cotter pins. Hitch manufacturers provide instructions for installing on various model trucks; these ensure that the hitch is installed in accordance with warranty requirements and over or in front of the rear axle. It's a good idea to have your hitch installed by an authorized dealer. If you are buying trailer and hitch together, you can probably get the dealer to install the hitch as part of the deal.

With the hitch installed, it's time to check the height adjustment. The best way to do this is to hitch up your trailer. Ideally the trailer should be close to level, front to back, when towed. At the same time there should be a minimum of six to eight inches of clearance between the truck side rails and the bottom of the forward section of the trailer. With less clearance you risk damage to truck, trailer or both when passing through dips such as you frequently encounter entering parking lots, driveways or below grade side roads. The upper part of the hitch can be raised to increase the clearance, and the pin box can also be adjusted up or down.

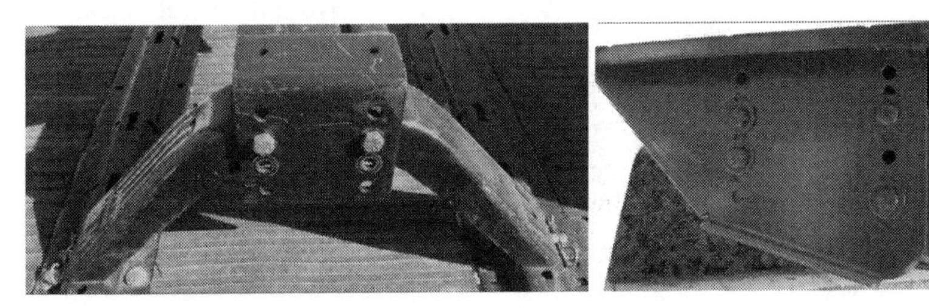

Height on both hitch and pin box can be adjusted to improve tow vehicle clearance.

With some high riding trucks such as four-wheel drive pickups, it may not be possible to obtain the clearance and still keep the trailer near level. If the fiver is too high in the front, it will cause contents to shift during travel and it may place excessive weight on the rear tires and axle. One solution to this dilemma is to "flip" the trailer axles if they are mounted above the leaf springs. In this procedure they are moved below, thereby raising the height of the trailer floor. If your axles are already below the springs, the height can be adjusted by inserting blocks between the axles and springs and securing with longer U-bolts.

Before we leave the subject of hitch installation, here's a suggestion. Your truck may be equipped with a seven-conductor towing receptacle mounted on the rear bumper. This would be fine for towing a conventional trailer, but for a fiver you want the receptacle mounted inside the bed, probably on the sidewall behind the driver's side wheel well. You can probably get that included with the hitch installation, or at least get both done at the same time. It's also a good time to have your brake controller installed. We'll discuss these devices in the next chapter, but you'll need it, so get it done now.

Fifth wheel hitches require little maintenance. The moving parts should be lubricated regularly to ensure smooth operation. Use a white lithium lubricant spray, try to reach into the interior areas, and operate the release handle to help distribute the spray. To lubricate the skid plate surface, an automotive chassis grease can be used; clean old grease periodically before applying more. Many fiver owners prefer to use a ten-inch Teflon plastic lube plate to avoid the mess and cleanup of grease. These plates are inexpensive and available at most RV supply stores. They are sized to fit snugly around the king pin so as to stay in place even when the trailer is unhitched. Replace them when damaged or when they become too worn to stay in place. Owners of sliding hitches will need to lubricate their slide rails according to manufacturer's instructions.

Hitching and un-hitching

Very little practice is required to master hitching and unhitching a fiver. A couple of key points make all the difference. When hitching, it is very important to adjust the trailer height correctly. Ideally the bottom plate on the trailer's pin box should be just below the top of the skid plate. Then as the truck is backed up, the pin box will ride up onto the skid plate, causing the truck bed to drop slightly as some of the trailer weight depresses the axle springs. This ensures proper vertical alignment. If the pin box comes in too high, the bottom of the king pin may rest on top of the hitch jaws or slide latch, resulting in a failure to capture the pin and possible damage to the mechanism. This is called high-pinning and must be avoided.

Tip - How to determine the approximate trailer height for aligning king pin with hitch: After you unhitch your trailer but before you raise or lower the landing gear to make it level, note how far your breakaway cable hangs above the ground. In my case it is usually about the width of the palm of my hand. When you are preparing to hitch, adjust the trailer height to return the cable to that position and you should be very close to the correct hitching height.

One more caution: Don't try to hitch by lowering the kingpin down into the center of the skid plate. If your alignment is off even slightly, the flange on the king pin can contact and damage the locking mechanism.

As the truck is backed farther under the trailer, the king pin is directed into the center of the hitch, causing the latching mechanism to open and then capture it. When the hitch arm snaps back into place, this indicates that the hitch is secured. With some hitches you may need to start with it unlatched.

Tip – Level your truck: If the truck is too far off level, you may experience problems aligning the hitch mechanism vertically with the king pin. Use leveling blocks, planks or even a Trailer-Aid ramp to level the truck as you back under the trailer.

Close the locking latch, hook up the breakaway cable and the electrical pigtail, close the tailgate, raise the trailer's landing gear and remove the wheel chocks. You may wish to place a padlock in the locking latch to deter anyone with vandalism in mind from releasing the hitch when you are away from the vehicle. We assumed at the outset of the hitching procedure that the trailer was already secured for travel, including all of the tasks listed in your Departure Checklist. You're ready to roll.

Tip – Test your hitch: After hitching, raise the landing gear until they clear the ground by a couple of inches. Then with wheel chocks still in place, manually apply the trailer brakes with the brake controller and put the truck in gear. If there is anything amiss and the hitch doesn't hold, you will find out without crushing the side rails of the truck bed. The trailer will simply drop onto the landing gear. Is there a sadder sight than a nice shiny truck with crushed side rails?

Unhitching is even easier than hitching. After chocking the trailer wheels, back the truck slightly to relieve pressure on the latching mechanism - just a nudge. Lower the landing gear until they are carrying most of the weight; the truck bed will stop rising. Open the tail gate, release the locking latch and disconnect the breakaway cable and pigtail. You're ready to drive the truck out from under the pin box. You can then proceed with leveling the trailer and complete your arrival routine.

Hauling with your tow vehicle

As we've noted, one of the benefits of owning a fifth wheel is having a truck available for hauling when it's not towing. Of course you can carry some loads with the hitch still in the truck bed, but for many chores removing the hitch makes sense. It provides more unobstructed haul capacity and may protect the hitch from possible damage.

All fiver hitches are removable, but the procedure will vary from one model to the next. They are all heavy however, weighing in excess of 100 pounds and in some models much more. In order to remove the hitch without straining a muscle, you will want to partially disassemble it, at least separating the hitch plate assembly from the base. Again, how this is accomplished will be different for various hitches, but the steps that I use when removing my Reese hitch should be instructive.

I begin by removing the large pivot pin that holds the plate assembly onto the base. I first have to remove the "klik pin" that acts as a retainer. I usually have to tap on the bottom of the pin to drive it out. I use the butt end of a handle or even a piece of 2x4 if it's handy. Now I can lift the entire plate assembly off the base. I replace the pivot pin in the base and secure it so that it doesn't get misplaced. Next I remove the spring cotter pins from the four pull pins and pop the pull pins out of the bed rails. I place the cotter pins back onto the pull pins for safe keeping. Now I lift the base off the rails and move it and the plate assembly to the tailgate. I am able to handle the base and plate assembly separately myself, but I know that some hitches, especially those with greater weight ratings, are significantly heavier. Save your back! Get help if yours is one of those. My rails are bolted to the frame and are not removable, but as we've noted, removable rails are available for some brands.

Tip – Lube your hitch: When you disassemble your hitch, you have the opportunity to give it quick checkup and lubrication. Flip over the plate assembly and inspect moving parts that are not normally visible or easy to reach with lubricants. Clean and spray where needed.

Replacing the hitch is just the reverse operation. I sometimes find it necessary to jiggle the base to align it with the holes in the bed rails, but the pins usually slip in easily. I lock in the pull pins, then replace the plate assembly onto the base. Again it may take a little adjusting to align the pivot hole so that the pivot pin can be inserted. Tapping is often necessary to get it started. The last step is to secure the pivot pin.

My Reese hitch disassembled for removing from truck bed.

Chapter 8 – Stuff: Options and Accessories

In Chapter 5 we offered some ideas on how to go about identifying the right fifth wheel for your needs and budget. We talked about some of the important factors that you should consider in your search. Even if you find the fiver of your dreams, it's likely that there will be some options that you may want to add. If you are ordering a unit from the factory, you'll want to take advantage of options that can be installed there. You'll probably get a better deal that way, they'll be included in your factory warranty and the work will probably be of better quality than if installed later. On the other hand, some options will probably not be available from the manufacturer, but you can probably buy most of them from an RV dealer and at a discount if you include them with the original trailer purchase.

Options

Here then are a few options to consider:

Slideout awning – You'll find some disagreement on this, but I have one on my slideout and recommend it. The main advantage is that it prevents debris from collecting on the roof of the slide. You won't have to remember to clean off your slide roof before retracting. An awning will also help protect the roof seal and may help eliminate leaks. The downside is that the awning flaps in a strong wind and can collect water during rain. At least one awning manufacturer makes a model with a center support that overcomes these problems.

Window awnings – Sometimes I wish I had these on a couple of my larger windows to reduce glare and heat on a hot sunny day.

Black tank spray nozzles – Just hook up a hose to the external inlet. Invaluable at keeping sewage from building up and keeping stuff moving when you are dumping. Sprays can also help keep your tank level sensors clean.

Trailer hitch receiver – If you want to tow a boat or utility trailer (in states where "triple-towing" is allowed), you'll want to have a hitch receiver. It's also a good way to install a bike rack.

Bicycle carrier – Bikes can be great for venturing out and exploring locally or just for getting around a campground. Trailer hitch mount and bumper mount designs are available.

V-cut flow-through tailgate – I had one of these on my first truck. I can't say for sure that it improved my gas mileage, towing or not, although they are supposed to help. But it is convenient to be able to hitch and unhitch without opening your tailgate. The reason I had one is that one fine day I got careless and tried to unhitch without lowering my original gate.

Inverter with deep cycle battery bank – Recommended for extended dry camping. Use all of your AC appliances except for air conditioner, microwave and electric coffee maker.

Generator – Your backup power supply when dry camping. With a running generator you can use the air conditioner and other power hungry appliances. Use it to recharge your batteries too. Avoid the cheap and noisy contractor units. If you use a generator, please be considerate of your neighbors and observe quiet hours.

Solar panels – Alternative energy for extended dry camping; used in conjunction with a bank of deep cycle batteries. Requires a charge controller to protect batteries from overcharge. With my 320 watts of solar panels I have dry camped for weeks.

Wind turbine – Another option for charging your batteries for free; great complement with solar - often the wind blows when the sun goes.

Accessories

OK, with trailer (now fully equipped), truck and hitch – you're good to go, right? Hold on now; before you hit the road, you need to go shopping - and not just for groceries. The list of essential accessories that are not included with a new trailer is extensive. My RV dealer included a $100 gift certificate with the purchase of the trailer, but it didn't go far when I started loading up on the stuff I would need.

The shopping lists that follow in the next couple of pages are mostly based on my experience; the first is for stuff you *will* need, followed by stuff that you can probably get along without, but that will make your travels a little easier or more pleasant. In my case, some stuff which I bought later on I catalog as essential. My advice: you'll need it eventually, so don't wait until it's a problem.

One more thing: Carry a tool box. You'll always have screws to tighten, minor repairs, etc., just like you would in a permanent dwelling. At a minimum, your tool box should include:

Hand tools: pliers, wrenches, screw drivers, small hammer
Socket set
Air pressure gauge

Bring along a battery powered electric drill too. And don't forget a good flashlight.

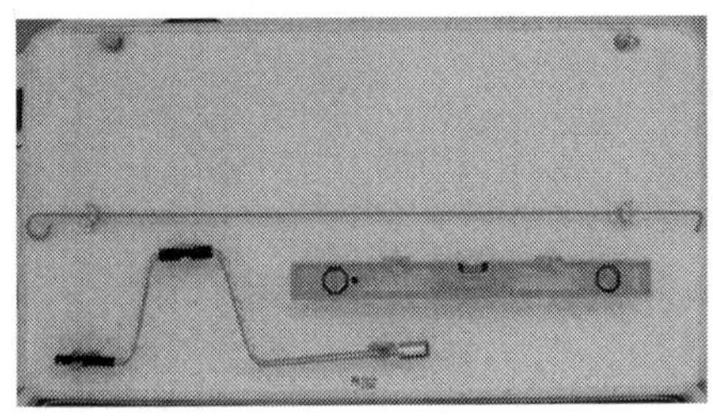

Tip – Organize your stuff: The cargo doors on a fiver are great for keeping tools, hoses and the like out of the way but readily accessible. Use nylon Velcro straps and closet tool holders to mount them.

Essential accessories	About and why you need them
Brake controller	Manual switch and improved control of trailer brakes; must for safety
Towing mirrors	These are larger and extend farther than normal side-mount mirrors. Another safety item. Usually available at auto dealers and parts stores.
Plastic hitch lube plate	Much easier than messing with grease.
Sewer hoses: two 10 foot sections	Hook up to campground sewer pipe; sometimes farther than 10 feet. Pick up a coupler too.
Sewer hose connectors	Get the clear plastic angle adapter for hooking hose to sewer connection and the 90° funnel adapter for connecting to sewer.
Water Pressure regulator	Needed to protect your low pressure internal plumbing from high pressure campground supply.
Water filter	Get a good one and ALWAYS filter all the water that goes into your rig.
Potable water hoses	Eliminates off-taste and odor that you may experience with a standard garden hose. Get two 25 foot lengths.
Water tank adapter	Put on the end of your water hose and stick in the inlet pipe.
Trailer-Aid wheel ramp	Makes changing a flat tire much easier, see next chapter.

Essential accessories	**About and why you need them**
Leveling indicators	Get two, for front and side.
Plastic leveling blocks	Get at least one set of these interlocking blocks. You'll use them with your landing gear, stabilizers or under the wheels.
Pair of 2x8 planks	Get these at your lumber yard, each 4 or 5 feet long. Very handy for leveling up wheels. Add in a couple of 10 or 12 inch square blocks in a couple of thicknesses for more flexibility.
Wheel chocks	Prevents trailer movement when hitching, unhitching or even at camp. Get Rotochocks or the plastic wedge-type. Or make your own by cutting 4x4 blocks at 45° on each end to fit between your tires.
Shelf/drawer liner non-slip mats	Get a roll of this and cut to fit your shelves and drawers. Keeps stuff from sliding around with normal highway bumps and sways.
Awning tie-down straps	Better than losing your awning in a wind storm.

Optional accessories	About and why you might want them
Under-sink water filter	Some water may have off-taste. With this filter you can use onboard water for drinking. Mine came with the trailer.
Gray water hose	If you get a sewage block, you don't want to use your potable hose to help unblock.
"Slinky" sewer hose stand	For a free draining hose. I have also seen ABS pipe cut down the middle and sections of roof gutter used to support sewer hose. I use a board and blocks.
Sewer hose carrier	Many trailers have a 4 inch steel tube rear bumper that holds sewer hose. If yours doesn't, get a carrier or make one out of 4 inch PVC pipe.
Blue "Tote-along"	Also called "blue boy." For hauling sewage to campground dump site when there's no sewer hookup at your site. Mine is 30 gal and can be towed behind my truck.
Rubber gloves	Wear when dumping. Some folks use disposables, but I find they tear easily. I use the kitchen type.
King pin stabilizer	This is typically a two or three legged support attached up front when parked to reduce sway and shaking. Some folks like them, but I haven't noticed the need on my fiver.
King pin lock	Ensures that no one can hitch up and abscond with your trailer while you are unhitched and away.

Optional accessories	About and why you might want them
Hydraulic jack	This is might be considered essential, but I have successfully changed tires using my Trailer-Aide and stabilizer jack. Recommended for heavier trailers.
Tire iron or torque wrench	You need to check your tire lugs every few thousand miles.
Pair of walkie-talkies	Great for improving communication with co-pilot when backing and parking.
Vent covers	I have MaxxAir covers installed over two of my vents, so I can leave the vents open when driving and during heavy rain.
Step covers	These wrap around your steps and help keep dirt out of the trailer
Door mat	Another dirt control measure, essential when you're camping in wet weather.
Astroturf type outdoor carpet	I don't use this, but lots of folks do. Keeps the dust down in your outdoor living area.
Awning screen-room	I don't have this either, but these are nice for enclosing the area under your awning as an "Arizona room."
Nylon Velcro straps – large	Useful for tying down or attaching lots of stuff.
Storage bins, various sizes	For organizing various accessories: water, sewer, electrical, etc.
Awning de-flappers	You may be surprised how much noise awnings can make in a steady wind, and how annoying it can be.

Optional accessories	About and why you might want them
Power adapters	Nice for plugging a 30 or 50 amp cord into a 20 amp outlet or a 50 amp cord into a 30 amp outlet. Note: 20 amps is fine for lights, charging batteries, and running the refrigerator or entertainment devices, but DO NOT run your air conditioner on 20 amps.
Inverter	With a small inverter you can charge your cell phone or run your computer on 12 volts. Not recommended for larger AC appliances. You'll need a 12-volt outlet in the trailer or use the one in your truck. For serious AC use when dry camped refer to Chapter 11.
Catalytic heater	Propane heater that uses no electricity. Furnace can drain your batteries when dry camping in colder weather.
Gutter spouts	These plastic gutter extenders can help eliminate black streaks from roof run-off. Very inexpensive and available at camping and RV stores.

Chapter 9 – Basic Fifth Wheel Skills

Are we there yet? Well, at least you're off the dealer's lot. If you've never towed or parked a fiver before, it's really a good idea to spend some time learning and practicing in a safe environment first. In this chapter we'll review the basic skills you'll need. In our next chapter we'll expand on these and cover highway safety.

Practice, practice, practice

The huge bulk of your fiver filling your rear view mirror the first time you tow can be a bit intimidating. Just getting your rig home from the dealer may introduce you to towing in traffic, making lane changes, turns and stop-and-go driving. Try to avoid heavy traffic and awkward situations until you have had a chance to work on your driving skills.

Plan on a couple of practice sessions on quiet weekdays or in low-traffic, open areas where you can work on your turns and get a feel for braking and stopping. Turn much wider when you are towing to provide clearance for the trailer coming around. Watch in your rear view mirror to make sure you don't take out any street signs as you take corners.

Next, work on your highway driving skills. These include passing, negotiating curves and grades, and managing your speed to meet traffic and driving conditions. You will be moving a lot of weight down the road, and it will take longer to crank it up and slow it down. Save steep mountain roads for later trips - start out with something easy. Get the feel of your brakes and how your rig handles curves. Take it slow and steady as you start out.

Tip – Back care: Do you carry your wallet in your back pocket? RVers frequently spend long hours sitting behind the wheel. Sitting on that wallet can be bad for your spine, causing one side of your body to sit higher than the other, and introducing spinal strain. Try driving with your wallet in a front pocket instead. You'll probably notice a difference.

Parking lots

Parking lots and shopping centers can present problems when you are towing. Try to scope out lots before entering to make sure that there is an easy exit and that you will have enough space to maneuver. You will probably need to take at least two parking slots, end-to-end, or up to five, six or more if you have to park across them. You'll find more space farther away from the main entrance and you're less likely to upset other shoppers by taking extra spaces closer in.

Backing and maneuvering

Some folks find backing a trailer intimidating, but it doesn't have to be. Learn a few simple techniques and you will be handling your rig like a pro. Take your fiver to an empty parking lot and practice mastering these skills. Use a couple of traffic cones or large plastic beverage bottles to help mark out spaces.

Simplify the task by thinking of it in four stages: initial positioning, starting the turn, following, and fine tuning. Ending up where you want to be is easier if you start in the right place, with the fiver wheels somewhat forward of the camp site, drive way or parking area. If you have a sliding hitch, now is the time to position it toward the rear.

Now put her in reverse and start the turn. The tendency is to place our hands at the top of the steering wheel, but if you learn instead to grip the wheel at the bottom when backing, you can avoid the confusion of reverse action. With your hand at the bottom of the wheel, move it left to turn the trailer to the left, and move right to steer it right - simple. So crank it hard in the direction you want to start the turn and slowly begin your turn.

Hand on the bottom of the wheel makes backing easier.

Once the turn is established and the trailer is pointed into the target area, turn the steering wheel in the opposite direction so that your front wheels are now aligned with the arc formed by the trailer and vehicle. You want your truck to follow the trailer in. Don't wait too long or you can jack-knife. If that happens, pull out and start over.

As you continue backing, keep an eye on the alignment of the trailer to the parking area. Keeping your hand on the bottom of the steering wheel, make small adjustments left or right as needed.

A co-pilot providing hand signals or coaching you via two-way radio, can be a big help. When you are parking at a camp site, you may need to get out and check your progress, especially if you are solo or your vision is obscured. Better to get out and look than to damage your trailer on an obstruction or overhead branch. If you start to get off track, pull forward and adjust. Don't try to over correct with large turns. As you continue backing, straighten out your truck to align it with the trailer and continue following it in. I promise, this will get easier with practice.

With turn established, follow the trailer in.

One thing to try to avoid is getting your truck at 90° to the trailer. This puts a lot of side pressure on the tires and could damage them or even force them off the rim.

When you are positioning your rig in an actual camp site, check for clearance for your slideouts. Often electrical power and fresh water hookup points are mounted on a short post along side the site. Avoid these as well as shrubs, tree limbs and large rocks that may also obstruct your slide.

Staying on the level

Leveling: it's something we have to do just about every time we park our rigs, but it's not difficult. The basic approach is first level side-to-side, then front-to-back. As you back or pull into your camp site, driveway or parking lot, stop when you are about where you want to be and take a first side-to-side level check. Externally mounted level indicators make this much easier; they are inexpensive accessories available at camping supply stores. With a large indicator mounted on your pin box, you may be able to check your side-to-side level without getting out of the truck. Determine if your rig is level or if you need to elevate one side or the other.

Externally mounted level indicators aid trailer leveling

You can use wood planks, interlocking plastic leveling blocks or even inflatable levelers to raise the low side of the trailer. Lay them on the ground, pull the trailer onto them and check your level again. You may need to repeat a couple of times, adding or removing blocks to get closer to level. With practice, this will get easier as you learn to calibrate the height adjustment needed. We don't need perfection, but try to get within about a half inch of level from one side to the other.

Wooden planks and wheel chock.

Now you can chock your wheels and prepare to unhitch. Always chock, even on a level surface. You don't want your trailer moving while unhitching.

Rotochock and plastic leveling blocks.

At this point make a first level check front-to-back. If your rig is high in the front, you may to need to extend your landing gear before you unhitch so that you have room to retract them again for final leveling. On the other hand, if you are quite low in the front, you may need to use blocks under your landing gear to avoid over-extending them to reach level.

Two types of landing gear, both on blocks.

Extend the landing gear and check when they make contact with the ground. You may need to shim up one or the other with blocks to keep your rig leveled side-to-side or to make a final tweak.

Now disconnect your breakaway cable and pigtail, then unhitch and pull the truck forward. Next retract or extend your landing gear to reach your final front-to-back level.

Congratulations! You're ready for the final step. Crank down your stabilizer jacks. Again you may need to use blocks if that end of your trailer happens to be too far above the ground. Snug up the stabilizers; use them to nudge the level slightly, but don't over do it. They aren't designed to carry the full weight of your trailer, only to reduce sway and shaking.

Two types of stabilizer jacks with elevating blocks.

If you are using a king pin stabilizer, now is the time to set it up. Although I don't use one, some owners say that they help eliminate rocking of the trailer when they are moving about inside. The king pin stabilizer can also include a lock, potentially deterring trailer theft.

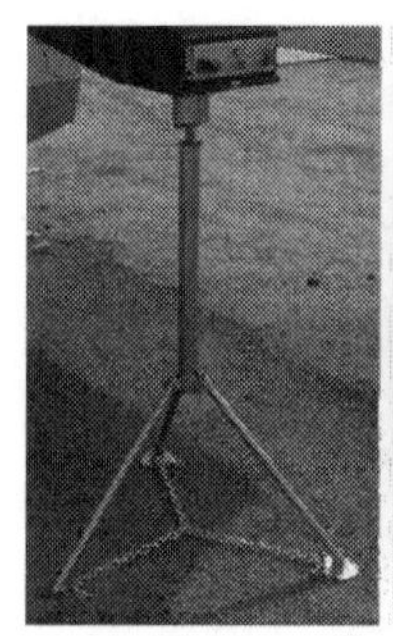

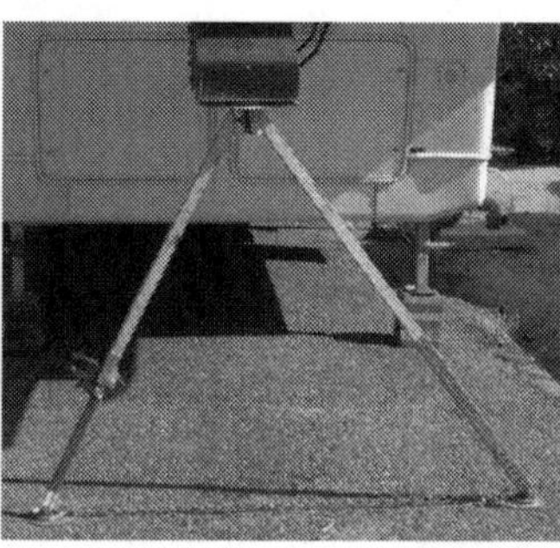

Three types of king pin stabilizers.

Camping Hitched

Occasionally and usually while you are in transit, you may be stopping for the night at a rest area or parking lot. Or you may just be spending one night at a campsite with plans to pull out and continue on the following day. In these situations I normally do not unhitch, provided that I can position the trailer so that it is reasonably level.

I will typically complete side-to-side leveling as if I were unhitching. I also will extend my landing gear so as to relieve the weight on my truck and improve stability. Since my rig tows just a little high in front because of the height of my 4x4 truck, on level surfaces I find it necessary to pull the trailer up on planks to get closer to level. I usually lower my stabilizer jacks when camping hitched to prevent rocking and raise the back end just a little.

Chapter 10 – On the Road with your Fifth Wheel

On the road at last! Before you head off to the mountains or seashore, let's make sure we get started off on the right track by taking a test drive. We're also going to cover some safety issues and talk about a few hazards that fifth wheelers may encounter. I'll admit to learning about some of these the hard way. Hopefully this chapter will help you avoid some of my mistakes.

Your shakedown cruise

Before you get carried away and take off on a two week or longer trip, it's a good idea to start a little closer to home with a shakedown trip.

Hopefully you left the RV dealer with all of your questions answered and with copious notes from your Pre-Delivery Inspection. Even if you had a very thorough walk-through with the sales or service team and had everything explained, there's still a lot to learn. Maybe you've also read the owner's manual cover to cover. However, only by actually operating the different systems can you discover what you don't know, but perhaps thought you did. Or find out what you don't have, but need.

Besides raising questions you didn't think of at the dealer, you'll find additional benefits to taking a short, get-acquainted trip in your new rig. Nearly every new trailer will have some warranty issues that can only be identified by taking your rolling home on the road and putting her through the paces. Better to find those problems when you're close to home, so you can get them fixed at your convenience and without the risk and hassle of working through a strange dealership.

A shakedown trip also helps you identify things that you forgot to pack or stock up on or that you didn't think you'd need. Then you can fill the cupboards and stock the pantry from your home supplies or local super markets. Stocking up at RV resorts or country stores can cost a bundle.

For your first trip, plan on about a three day outing, certainly no more than a week. If dry camping will be part of your lifestyle, then plan to spend a night or two without hookups. Learning how your fresh and waste water systems operate is essential, so plan on staying at a park or resort with hookups too. In Chapter 11 we'll go over these systems in more detail.

Try everything out and take notes on any problems that you encounter. After you get home, take your list of issues down to your dealer and get everything resolved.

Brakes

Your trailer has its own set of brakes, electrically controlled via the heavy pigtail cable that you connect to your truck. Hopefully, you have also had a brake controller installed to improve your braking performance and to provide a manual switch for activating the trailer brakes apart from your truck brakes. Adjust the brake controller following the manufacturer's instructions. Then try stopping both normally and more suddenly as you might need to in an emergency. You may need to fine tune the controller settings to improve your braking performance.

As a safety precaution, fifth wheels are also equipped with a breakaway cable that you must remember to attach to the truck every time you hitch up. I loop mine over the hitch handle. In case your hitch should fail while driving, the cable will pull out and engage a switch to immediately activate the trailer brakes. An out of control trailer veering down the highway would be a terrifying prospect.

Finally, remember to have your trailer brakes checked annually or every 3,000 miles.

Driving Grades

Unless your RV travels are limited to coastal areas or the Midwest, sooner or later you are going to face driving grades. On the way up grades can cause overheating and drive train wear and tear, while the down hill run poses the risks of burning brakes and losing control. By using your drive train effectively, you can make the drive on both sides of the mountain easier and safer.

Although your actions will differ depending on whether your truck has a manual or automatic transmission, the approach is the same: On the ascent you want to keep your engine and drive train operating in the most effective range of its power curve. Heading down you want to use the drive train to help maintain control while using your brakes judiciously.

Mountain grades lead to wonderful places. By Russ & Tina De Maris

Optimal engine speed and gear selection for any particular grade will depend on your engine size and type - gasoline or diesel – your transmission – manual or automatic - and your gear ratio. Regardless, on the ascent keep your RPMs in the power range by downshifting as necessary. Start by trying to build up some speed and dropping out of overdrive as you approach the slope, and if you are going to be in the mountains for a while, stay out of overdrive. With an automatic you may not have to do anything else, just let the transmission take over. If your automatic has a Tow-Haul mode, use it. With a manual, downshift whenever your tachometer indicates that you are in the lower part of your power range. Watch the engine temperature. Be prepared to pull off where it is safe to do so to prevent over heating, and if you do, leave the engine running for a few minutes to keep your coolant circulating. Then turn it off and let it cool. If you have a temperature gauge on your transmission, watch it also; you don't want to ruin your fluid by letting it hold above about 250° F for any length of time. Again, pull off and idle to avoid overheating.

Heading down the other side, it's all about control. If there are curves, holding down your speed is essential for safety. The longer and steeper the grade, the more you will want to use your drive train to help control your speed. Using brakes alone can cause them to overheat and lose their effectiveness when you most need them. On grades of 6% or less, running with overdrive disengaged may be sufficient, but steeper hills will likely require lower gears. This will vary with your weight and vehicle; you'll learn as you gain experience, but start slow. With an automatic transmission you will probably need to drop it into lower gears yourself. Keep an eye on your engine speed and use your brakes to avoid red-lining. Applying your brakes in short bursts will help keep them cool. Use the manual switch on your brake controller to alternate between braking with the trailer brakes and truck brakes.

These are general ideas. Be sure to read your owners manual for any specific driving instructions that the manufacturer recommends.

Narrow roads and sharp turns

Take sharp turns wide. When driving a car, my tendency is to cut sharp corners close to the inside edge. Towing a fifth wheel, this can be disastrous. I cut a turn too sharply towing on a narrow mountain road and whacked my fifth wheel on a vertical rock escarpment. I was lucky that my awning took the force of the blow. The trailer wasn't damaged, but the awning was destroyed - thankfully my insurance covered it. Cutting a sharp curve with a drop off below could be even worse if your rear tires don't make the turn. Pull wide through those curves so that your rig can track well on the roadway.

Ruined awning from taking a mountain turn too sharply

Driveways and side roads

Some driveways, parking lot entrances and side roads can present a problem as you turn into them. Often the main road slopes down toward its edge and the driveway or entrance slopes up the other side, resulting in a "valley." As the truck starts down the valley, the trailer is still level. If the sides of the valley are steep enough, the back corner of the truck side rails may come into contact with the underside of the trailer, possibly damaging either or both. Similarly, as the truck starts up the other side of the valley, the trailer is still heading downhill. The front of the trailer can contact the side rails, again risking body damage to either or both. In Chapter 7 we mentioned this in connection with hitch height and clearance between truck and trailer. With good clearance you won't face this problem often, but you should be aware of it. If you do start into a steep side turn, watch in your rear view mirror and try to adjust the turn so as to avoid making contact.

Watch your stabilizers

When fully retracted my stabilizer jacks extend just 4 ½ inches below the rear bumper, but they can still drag in some circumstances. Steep driveways are one hazard, as are deep road dips. I have also learned to pay attention when backing into uphill sloping camp sites or those bordered by large rocks. I've had to replace my stabilizers a couple of times. They are available at camping supply stores and, in my case at least, they are bolted on, so not difficult to swap out.

Tire safety is important

Your trailer rides on air – the air pressure in your tires. If pressure is too high or too low, tires will overheat, wear unevenly, and possibly even blow out. The recommended cold inflation pressure for your tires is indicated on the trailer

Low tire pressure leads to uneven wear and tire failure.

certification label (see Chapter 5) or in your owner's manual. You can also check the tire inflation chart for your particular tire, available from the tire manufacturer. Check your tires' air pressures at least monthly and before each trip.

One more point: under inflated tires can adversely affect your fuel mileage.

Changing a flat tire is pretty straight forward. I use a Trailer-Aid ramp to provide several inches of easy "jacking" – just pull the trailer up on to it. Its curved top also acts as a chock, but chocking the wheels on the opposite side is also necessary. I still need a couple of extra inches in order to fit the new tire on, but I can get this by cranking up the rear stabilizer or landing gear (depending upon which tire I'm changing). With a heavier trailer I recommend carrying and using a hydraulic jack to lift the trailer frame. Tighten the lug nuts to the recommended torque and then check them again within the next 50 miles.

Spare tire mounted with help of Trailer-Aid.

Check your weight

Back in Chapters 4 and 6 we talked about weight ratings of trailers and tow vehicles, GCVR and GVWR, and why they are important. But what's really important is your actual weight. Here's how you can find out whether or not you have a weight problem.

If you are fortunate enough to attend an RV rally where the Recreation Vehicle Safety Education Foundation is offering free wheel-by-wheel weighing, try to take advantage of the opportunity. Some RV dealers also offer weight-by-wheel services. This is the definitive way to check your weights and the only way to check the balance of your trailer by axle and side-to-side. Add up the weight on each wheel to validate your axle weights as well as gross vehicle and combined weights.

Lacking wheel-by-wheel weights, you can still check your combined, vehicle and axle weights if you can locate an idle highway weight station, or maybe a friendly one that's not too busy. You'll need to weigh your tow vehicle separately, including a full load of fuel and the normal complement of passengers. Then with your trailer in tow, weigh your truck again, first all four wheels, then pull forward and record the rear axle weight only. Next, drive forward so the trailer wheels are on the scale and record the weight. Now do some arithmetic.

Truck Gross Vehicle Weight = Truck weight (hitched)

Truck Gross Axle Weight = Truck rear axle (hitched)

Truck Gross Combined Weight = Truck weight (hitched) plus Trailer weight

Pin Weight = Truck weight (hitched) minus Truck weight unhitched

Trailer Gross Vehicle Weight = Trailer weight plus Pin weight

Approximate Trailer Gross Axle Weight for two axle trailer = Trailer weight divided by 2. Divide by 3 for three axles.

Check your actual weights against your weight ratings. An overweight trailer is subject to excessive brake, tire and axle wear. From a safety perspective, it is more difficult to maintain control on down grades and your stopping distance is greater. If you should have an accident while towing and you are found to have been overloaded, you may face a citation and insurance problems.

Chapter 11 – Hookups, Dry Camping and a Lot More

In this chapter we'll cover subjects that are not really unique to fifth wheels, but which should be of interest to new fiver owners. As traveling homes, our rigs come with their own utilities: power, water and sewage. How you use them will depend in part on whether you are staying at a park with hookups or dry camping. We'll cover both situations and talk about some other camping related topics.

Hooking up

Let's start with a review of hookups. Depending on where you are camping, you may find water only, water and electrical (shore) power, or all three types of hookups available. One of the things to pay attention to as you set up at a site is the position of the various hookup sources. Since the connection points on your rig are on the left (driver's) side, most of the time you'll want to park with the sources on that side. It's not much trouble to hook up to water or power from the other side, but it can be a hassle trying to hookup to sewer that way. Also make sure that your power cord and hoses will reach the hookups before you unhitch.

Tip – Hookup order: Start with power while your hands are dry. Next hookup water while your hands are clean. Last hookup to sewer; then clean up. I recommend this order even if you wear gloves as I do.

Hooking up to power is pretty simple – plug in both ends. To be on the safe side, turn off the breaker at the power box before plugging in. Tighten the sealing ring at the connector to your trailer, then turn on the juice. Hopefully you will have power available in the capacity you need, 30 or 50 amps. Occasionally you may find only 20 amp power available, so I recommend carrying an adapter. Remember, 20 amps is fine for lights, charging batteries, and running the refrigerator or entertainment devices, but DO NOT run your air conditioner on 20 amps. You can probably run your microwave if you're not using much power elsewhere.

Water hookup is also very simple. The most important thing to remember is to use a pressure regulator between the supply and your water inlet. Your trailer's water plumbing is a low pressure system. Some campground water supplies are at high pressure and a blown joint inside your rig could be pretty messy. It's also important to use potable water hose to prevent off-taste in your water. In addition I recommend always filtering any water that goes into your trailer. I've seen a surprising amount of crud collect on my ceramic filter at what I expected to be a clean supply. To save money, some folks choose to buy filters from home supply stores and adapt them for use with their RV. Another suggestion: flush a little water out of the spigot before attaching your regulator or hose; there might be a spider or some other debris up in there. Then flush any stale water out of your hose and filter. And finally, when you stow your hose, drain any water out, then coil it up and attach the ends to keep bugs and dirt out.

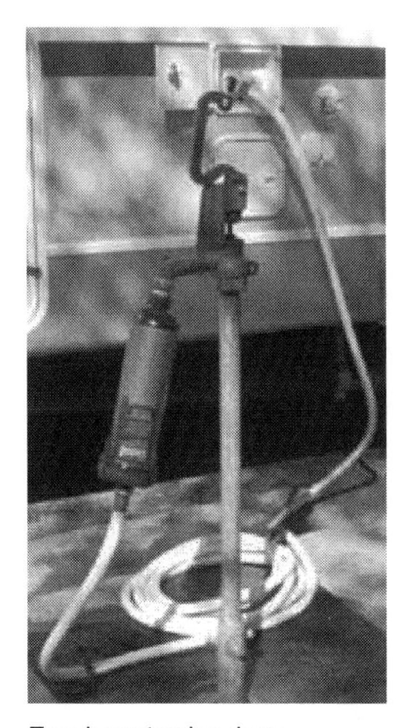

Fresh water hookup

Tip – Avoid freeze-ups: In cold weather, rely on your onboard water supply. Disconnect and drain your water hose to avoid damage to it or to your filter caused by freezing.

Hooking up to sewer may be just a little more involved. The fittings are easy enough to use; just slide on and turn to tighten. As shown in the photograph, a transparent adapter let's you see the flow so you know when the drain is empty or a blockage may have occurred. At the other end, it works best if you use a cone adapter rather than just poking the end of your hose down the sewer pipe. Not only is this unsanitary, it's easy for the hose to come out and leave you

With a transparent adapter you can see what's happening.

with a mess. With the adapter, you can place a rock or brick on the cone flange to keep it tight to the sewer pipe and minimize odors. Along its length you want to support your drain hose by some means to avoid low sections where fluids or solids can collect. Try to achieve a steady slope. You can use a board on blocks or buy a "slinky" drain hose

Slinky and rain gutters support the drain hose to achieve good flow.

support. Some RVers use sections of rain gutter; it's light weight, and two sections can be telescoped easily to extend their reach.

Tip – Use a bucket: Before you remove the cap on your sewage pipe, place a bucket beneath it. If your black tank valve leaks at all, you could have some amount of waste water collected in the line. Better to catch it in the bucket than have a mess to clean up.

We'll cover dumping your tanks soon. For now just remember that when hooked up you do not want to leave your black tank valve open. A volume of liquid is required to flush solid and paper residues out of the tank and down the drain lines. Normal flushing won't provide enough flow and will result in an accumulation of solids that can be very difficult to remove later. So keep the valve closed until you are ready to dump. It is OK to leave your gray tank valve open while hooked up.

Dry camping

As a matter of semantics, *dry camping* refers to living in your rig without hookups, regardless of location. You can dry camp in a Wal-Mart lot or in a forest in the middle of nowhere. Either way you are going to be relying on the onboard systems that make for comfortable, self-contained living. To get the most out of your stay, start with conservation. When you dry camp, you need to mentally "shift gears;" think about your power, fresh water and your gray and black tanks as limited resources.

Dry camping in a National Forest.

Eliminate waste

Starting again with electrical power, when you are "off the grid" you will relying on your 12-volt batteries for lights and electrical needs. Even if you have a generator, it's just not practical to run it all of the time you are camping. We'll discuss solar and generator power options below, but our purpose here is to suggest some ways to help you get the most out of your batteries. The deep cycle batteries used in RVs are designed to be cycled hundreds of times, but their lifetime will be considerably shortened if they are allowed to discharge much beyond half of their rated capacity. So it pays to conserve.

Rule number one: avoid using your battery power to produce heat, whether that heat is for hot water, coffee or other 12-volt appliances. It takes a lot of watts to make a little heat. So make sure that you use the LP switch for your water heater; turn off the electrical switch if you have one.

While your furnace uses propane for heat, its blower draws a substantial amount of current. So if you're going to need heat, consider a catalytic heater instead. These units burn propane very efficiently and use no power at all. You will need to crack a window though, to provide some fresh air. And never use your oven or stove top for the purpose of heating your rig. Don't forget to set your refrigerator to run on LP.

Your 12-volt lighting doesn't draw much power, but it makes sense to turn on only the lights you will need. For reading it might be better to use a small portable reading lamp.

A catalytic heater requires no electricity.

If your trailer is equipped with an inverter for producing 120 volt AC from battery power, here are a few more pointers. Inverters are only about 80% efficient, so try to minimize your use of AC and turn off the inverter when you are not using any AC appliances. The first rule still applies, so instead of using a regular coffee maker, use a tea kettle on the stove to heat water for coffee or tea. A French press makes great coffee or just use a cone filter. Hair dryers are another heat producing appliance whose use should be minimized. Your microwave will also pull lots of power, so use it sparingly. Turn off the inverter at night so that so called parasitic loads (TV, microwave and other AC appliances with standby capabilities) don't continue to draw power.

Do not run your air conditioner on inverted battery power. It will drain a large bank of batteries in a very short time and can easily burn out the compressor motor. A generator is the only option if you need air conditioning while dry camping.

Water Conservation

Water should never go down the drain unused. Collect water from sink or shower when waiting for it to get hot. Catch it in a pitcher, then use it to brush your teeth, make coffee, cook or even to flush the commode.

Adopt "Navy showers:" get wet, turn off the water while soaping, rinse, turn off again to shampoo, rinse again. Use only as much water as you need. If your shower doesn't have a quick shutoff, you can find one at your home improvement store. Capture the rinse water from dish washing in a plastic tub. Dishwater should not be dumped on the ground, but rinse water is fine.

Filling your fresh water tank

Of course if you are planning to dry camp, you want to start with a full tank of fresh water. Filling your supply tank is a lot like hooking up. You don't need the pressure reducer, but otherwise, hook up your hose and filter and flush them as before. Then insert the hose into the water inlet and fill. Before you fill the first time, sanitize your tank and water plumbing as described in Chapter 12 or your owner's manual. Some campers carry bottled drinking water and only use the water in their tank for washing and flushing. Our experience is that most of the time sanitizing, filtering the water you put in the tank, and using an under-sink charcoal filter will result in clean, drinkable water.

For longer stays, replenish your fresh water supply. One option is to break camp and take your rig to where water is available. However, you can bring water to camp. Options here include:

- water bladders that can be carried in the truck bed
- one or more five-gallon poly containers
- 50 gallon poly barrels for potable water available from some water bottling plants

You'll need a funnel or a hose to transfer the water into your fresh water tank. A small pump for use with a drill may also come in handy if you're not able to use gravity to siphon the water.

Drill pump for transferring fresh water.

Dumping

These suggestions apply whether you are emptying your tanks at an RV dump site or on sewer hookup at a campground. First, always start with your black (sewage) tank. It's best to let your black tank fill at least half way before dumping it, even when you are camped with hookups. This allows solids and tissues to partially break down and liquefy so that they will flow easier. It also results in a heavier flow that will help carry material out of the tank, down the drain piping and out the hose.

Follow by dumping your gray tanks. This way the soapy gray water will help to clean your sewer hose by flushing residues and sudsing drainage surfaces. Following the gray water dump, flush your fittings and hoses with water and always remember to hose off the dump area. Leave it for the next camper as you would like to find it yourself. Finally, partially fill your black water tank with clean water, perhaps a quarter of the way. Liquid in the tank will aid the breakdown of paper and solids and help prevent any build up.

Hauling waste water

To avoid pulling up stakes when your gray or black tank gets full, you can use a portable sewage "tote" to carry waste

Filling and dumping a "blue boy."

water to a dump site. Wheeled totes can be towed at slow speed to a dump point within a campground, but for hauling longer distances, you'll need to get the tote into your truck. In that case remember that water is heavy. Only drain as much into the tote as you can load without strain. Some RVers use macerator pumps to move waste water directly to a tote in their truck bed. Try searching online for more information on this approach.

Before we leave this subject, don't even think about dumping your tanks out in wilderness areas, even gray water.

Generators, Solar and Wind Power

Unless dry camping stays are limited to no more than a couple of days, an ancillary electrical power supply is essential. The options are: generators, photovoltaic (PV) solar and wind turbines.

Generators have the advantage that you can have your power wherever and whenever you want it. Just plug your power cord into the generator's outlet. In practice however, many parks and campgrounds limit the amount of time that generators are allowed to be operated. The problem is noise; newer models are well muffled, but still very audible to any nearby campers who are enjoying the outdoors or just have their windows open. Older contractor-grade generators are not recommended – too noisy. They are a sure fire way to upset anyone camped near you. Other negatives: obviously generators require fuel and if you use them extensively, you either need to carry a lot or make fuel runs when you run low. The exhaust fumes they produce can also be objectionable to folks trying to enjoy the clean air of natural surroundings.

To get the most out of a generator, plan on expanding your battery capacity so that you can store power for the hours when you don't or can't run it. And if you want to use AC appliances during those off hours, look into an inverter. You'll need to size the battery bank and the inverter to your needs. Batteries are heavy though; my inverter and batteries probably reduce my cargo capacity by 300 pounds.

Inverter and four deep cycle batteries fit in front storage compartment.

For campers who relish complete independence in the outback or who just want to avoid the noise, exhaust and fuel issues of generators, solar may be the answer. As long as the sun shines, PV panels silently capture the sun's energy. Solar panels have continued to increase in efficiency over the years, and they are now a viable option for RV electrical power sources. Panels in 80 and 120 watt sizes easily fit on the roof of most fivers and in pairs or as a set of 4 you can build systems of up to 240 or 480 watts.

PV panels collecting free electricity. The “remote” panel adds flexibility.

The other essential for a solar powered fiver is a charge controller to protect the deep cycle batteries. Again, you need to size the solar array and the battery bank to your anticipated needs. As with generators, an inverter added to your system will allow you to run AC appliances. Advising on solar sizing, configurations and installation is beyond our scope. However, many solar equipment retailers provide worksheets to help you size your system. They can install for you or provide instructions for doing the work yourself.

Small turbines harness the wind. Courtesy Southwest Windpower, Inc.

In some locations it may be difficult to find a camp site with full sun all day, and even in the sunniest climes, it is possible to have several days of limited sun. For the solar powered RV, this could spell trouble: time to head for home or at least a hookup. Increasingly, small wind turbines are being added to the arsenal of energy independent campers. At under $500, easy to erect, hook up and maintain, they can often pick up the slack on cloudy days and they work at night.

Awnings

Awnings are great for providing shady spot to relax and a dry area outside the trailer on wet days. They can also help keep things cool inside on a hot sunny day.

An awning provides shade and shelter.

Rolling your awning out is fairly simple: release the locking lever and latches, use the awning rod to reach the pull strap and unroll the awning, lock in the rafter arms and then raise the main arms. Optionally, you can unlatch the main arms and set them up vertically so you don't have to duck around them. If you do so, you'll need to anchor them with a couple of spikes or tent stakes. Always keep one end of the awning lower than the other so that any rain will run off. Too much weight could result in a collapse.

De-flapper fastened to rafter arm.

It's a good idea to use tie-down straps to help

protect awnings from freak strong winds. But if there's even a reasonable chance that a storm with winds is on the way, it's best to take your awning down. In even moderate winds an awning may flap, which can become very annoying. Inexpensive "de-flappers" are available and easy to use.

Taking an awning down is just the reverse process. Lower the main and rafter arms, take a firm grip on the pull strap, release the locking lever, and use the awning rod to maintain control of the awning as it rolls up. Secure the latches.

If you have to retract your awning wet, remember to roll it out again later to dry out and prevent mildew from starting.

Online on the road

There are many reasons to use the Internet while traveling. Besides email for staying in touch, the net can provide weather forecasts, access to banking and finances, route planning, reserving ahead for campsites and other attractions, and even telecommuting. Getting online away from home has become a lot easier in recent years. The choices include old fashioned dial-up service, cell-based, wireless (wifi) and satellite services. Each has differing costs and particular advantages, but satellite internet service is the only option that works from virtually anywhere.

Dial-up service may suffice if you only go online occasionally and you don't need higher speed service. Many campgrounds provide phone connections along with other hookups. However, to avoid long distance charges, you will need to ensure that your Internet Service Provider (ISP) offers toll free or local access phone numbers for the area where you are staying.

Various cell-based Internet services are available including nation-wide broadband plans. You need to be within a service area to take advantage of these. One advantage is that the service can be used in motion.

Wireless Internet is growing in popularity. Many campgrounds, including some state parks, now offer wifi access, as do some truck stops. Wireless is a relatively high speed service, much faster than dial-up. Most newer laptops include a built-in wireless adapter; add-on adapters are fairly inexpensive. Some campgrounds include wifi in their base site rental while others charge extra. National wifi service plans are available, but there is no guarantee that your plan will be honored at any particular location. Another consideration: quality of service can vary depending upon your distance from the site access point or antenna.

Satellite internet service is relatively high speed and available nearly everywhere. Options include fully automatic, roof-mounted systems and manual tripod mounts that must be set up and pointed at each camp site. Service availability is limited only by the "footprint" of your assigned satellite, something to check when signing up. Typical footprints cover major areas of the US and beyond. You also need line-of-sight to your assigned "bird." In some cases this will mean finding a "hole in the trees;" manual tripod systems offer more flexibility in that regard.

With satellite you can get online from almost anywhere.

Chapter 12 – Maintenance Chores

The joy of home ownership – on wheels. Just as with any other domicile, a fifth wheel requires a certain amount of regular maintenance. Your owner's manual should provide details on most of the various components and systems on your fiver. If they recommend something different that we do here, be sure to follow their advice. Our purpose here is to call to your attention the most common maintenance items and offer suggestions. Some of these have been covered previously in various parts of this book, but it seems like a good idea to gather all of this information in one place.

Recommended fifth wheel maintenance

Hitch - Periodically lubricate all of the moving parts with a white lithium lubricant spray and replace the lube plate when it becomes so worn that it won't stay on the king pin. If you have a sliding hitch, lubricate the slide rails according to manufacturer's instructions.

Roof and exterior - Since different types of roof and exterior wall materials are used by various fifth wheel manufacturers, there's no one-size-fits-all recommendation. EPDM rubber roofs should be washed annually with an approved cleaning solution and a soft brush. Most sidewalls can be cleaned with any gentle detergent and a soft brush. Wax periodically using a wax appropriate for the finish on your trailer. Fivers are subject to two problem areas: black streaks from roof run-off and bug splatter on the front. These take a little more elbow grease and possibly a stronger detergent; non-abrasive scrubbing pads help. Inexpensive plastic gutter extenders can help eliminate streaks.

Inspect your roof for leaks at least annually and use an appropriate patching or repair material to seal any suspect or damaged areas.

Slideouts - Periodically lubricate all of the moving parts with a white lithium lubricant spray and treat the rubber seals with a spray conditioner. Check the slideout roof seals every time you check your roof and remember to remove any debris before retracting your slides.

Brakes – Most trailer brakes are not self-adjusting. Have them inspected and adjusted annually or every 3,000 miles. Replace when worn.

Wheel bearings - Repack annually or every 6,000 miles.

Wheel lug nuts - Tighten to recommended torque every 3,000 miles and within 50 miles after changing a tire.

Tires - Inspect and check air pressure at least monthly and before each trip.

Fresh water tank - Before using your fresh water supply tank for the first time, make sure to sanitize it. If you don't use your fresh water tank for an extended period of time, it's a good idea to sanitize it again before refilling. Also, if the water from your tank develops an unpleasant taste or odor, it's probably time to re-sanitize.

With your water heater off, drain the tank. For every15 gallons of tank capacity make up a solution of ¼ cup of household bleach per gallon of water. Pour into your tank using a funnel, then fill the tank with water. Turn on the pump and flush water out all faucets and the shower. Let stand 3 hours. Drain and flush. Then sweeten the tank with a solution of one quart vinegar per five gallons of tank capacity. Flush water out of all faucets and drain. Then fill with fresh water. Or follow instructions in your owner's manual.

Black (sewage) tank - You will find some disagreement on this subject. Most folks agree that treatments are necessary, but some argue that you need to use harsh chemicals, often containing formaldehyde, in order to control odors. My experience is that enzyme-based treatments are better. A good one will control odor and promote digestion and rapid breakdown of paper products and solid wastes. Formaldehyde treatments destroy enzymes and beneficial bacteria and are harmful to sewage systems where they are dumped. Some RV dumps prohibit the use of formaldehyde-based treatments. Add the treatment after every dump, or as directed on the container.

Gray (bath and kitchen) tank - Little maintenance is required, but occasional use of an enzyme treatment can help eliminate odors and scum accumulation. Pouring into drains will also help keep your P-traps clear.

Batteries - Even maintenance free batteries require some attention. Keep all batteries clean and free of corrosion; clean the terminals and coat with a battery terminal spray. Check the water level on standard batteries on a regular basis. The level should be up to the bottom of the fill port, and when necessary topped up with distilled water.

SAFETY NOTE: All batteries produce hydrogen gas, which, if ignited can cause injury or death. Batteries contain strong acid which is also hazardous. Use care when working around batteries, and if you're not comfortable, refer the service to a qualified service professional.

Storage – Unless you are a full timer, it's likely that you may be putting your unit in storage from time to time. Your owners manual will probably have specific advice on this, but in general there are a few steps you'll need to follow: Disconnect your batteries so they don't drain due to parasitic loads, such as detectors. Drain and flush your waste tanks. If freezing temperatures are a possibility, either a) drain the fresh water, water heater and all of your lines or b) add antifreeze to your fresh water tank, install the water heater bypass and run water though your faucets to circulate the antifreeze solution.

Random advice

Here are a few tips that I've learned along the way, but which don't seem to fit in other sections of this book.

Bungees - Heavy items stored in cabinets with forward facing doors could be at risk if you need to stop quickly. They may slam against a door and, if the latch doesn't hold, come flying out. As a precaution, use bungee cords to help hold doors closed in transit. Get the kind with plastic ends to avoid marring your cabinetry.

Storage compartment locks - The original exterior storage compartment locks on most RVs are all keyed the same. Inexpensive replacement locks are available at most RV supply stores and many locksmiths. While a determined thief can still break into most storage compartments with a pry bar, changing your locks will provide some protection against casual theft.

Rituals - I have a tendency to forget to stow my steps or my handrail after using my trailer at a rest stop. I developed a little ritual to help me remember to secure them. My stairs have 3 steps, so now when I walk down those steps, I use them to jog my 1-2-3 ritual: 1 - close door, 2 - stow handrail, 3 - stow stairs. We have a lot to remember with our rigs and sometimes a lot on our minds when traveling. Creating simple memory devices like this can help you remember important details.

Chapter 13 – Fifth Wheeling in the Back Country

Congratulations! Since you've come this far, you have all the basic information you need to be able to tow, park and enjoy living aboard your fifth wheel trailer. If you plan to spend your camping time in established campgrounds at private RV parks and local, state or national parks, this chapter may not be for you. But you might as well come along for the ride – We're going boondocking!

What is Boondocking?

Unfortunately, this term means different things to different folks. Some use it synonymously with dry camping, even to mean staying in a Wal-Mart or Home Depot parking lot. The word boondocking derives from *boondocks*: "rural country, the backwoods, a remote and undeveloped area." So for our purposes *boondocking* refers to staying at an undesignated, probably undeveloped, and generally remote site, while as we have previously established, *dry camping* means no hookups, but in a designated area or developed site or lot.

Why Boondock?

My primary motivation is quality of the experience. I've stayed at many nice campgrounds, but very few offer the solitude and scenery of the wild places that I prefer. Finding and enjoying such places is really why I chose to take up the RV lifestyle in the first place.

Secondarily, for me at least, keeping my RV costs as low as possible is important. I need to take advantage of low cost ($5 a day is common at many locations) or free camping to help counter the high price of diesel fuel.

Camp for free ... Where?

Here's the deal: You can camp for up to two weeks, sometimes longer, at no charge on U.S. public lands (BLM areas, National Forests and some Wildlife Refuges) unless camping is specifically restricted. Stated the other way round, if it doesn't say you can't, then you can. So how do you go about finding good camp sites in these areas?

In some cases the responsible agencies operate designated campgrounds, some of which include amenities like fire rings, picnic tables and even pit toilets, but which are still free. You can often find these listed in publications such as Don Wright's "Guide to Free Campgrounds" or possibly online at www.FreeCampgrounds.com. In addition you can inquire at local or district Forest Service or BLM offices.

However, free designated campgrounds are the exception. In most cases you'll need to search out dispersed camp sites on your own. Finding these usually means getting off the beaten track, locating Forest Service and BLM roads, and doing a little exploring. Many of the best sites are found on secondary roads, so good maps are essential. We carry a large format road and recreation atlas/gazetteer for each state where we intend to camp. We like both the Delorme and Benchmark atlases. National Forest maps from the Forest Service are also excellent. You can often find them at sporting goods stores or fly and tackle shops near the area or obtain them at district offices and ranger stations.

I should note here that probably the best areas for boondocking are in the West. There is just a lot more empty and public land available. I would love to explore the eastern sections of the country at some time, but for now, my experience is limited to the mountain and Pacific coast states.

Getting there

A word of caution: These back roads can be narrow, steep or rough. You probably won't be able to tell by looking at a map whether a road is appropriate for towing your fiver. Reversing direction with a fiver in tow requires considerable room to maneuver. It's best to approach these roads with care.

Here are some tips:

Steep hills and canyons usually have narrow roads, where it may be hard to turn around.

Find a good spot to unhitch and lock your rig, then explore the area in your truck.

Unless you drive a four wheel drive truck, you should probably stick to paved roads or major arteries; certainly avoid steep spurs and side roads, loose gravel and mud.

Take it slow and, if necessary, scout ahead on foot before getting yourself stuck.

A tight squeeze.

On one of my earlier forays into the National Forest backwoods, I nearly wedged myself three times in one day. The secondary roads I was exploring became narrower with turnouts and spurs farther apart. One dead-ended, forcing a very tight turn around. The other two roads continued, but with no prospects in sight. I eventually backed my fiver up into spurs and managed to jockey enough to complete the u-turns. I mangled a stabilizer in the process. The other choice in such cases is to back your rig out of trouble, not easy either on a narrow gravel road. I now follow the advice provided above whenever I have any doubts.

Even on main roads it pays to be a little cautious. New Mexico State Highway 567 west of Taos looks innocuous enough on the map, indicating a gravel section of a few miles at the Rio Grande Gorge. Approaching it, we came to the precipice overlooking the canyon and had to catch our breath. Beyond lay a very steep and washboarded stretch of road with extreme hairpin turns descending into the abyss. We backed up to a level area, parked the trailer, and, after looking over the situation, took an alternate route.

The Goal

What you are looking for is a reasonably level spot, preferably away from any traffic, with room to maneuver. Ideally your site should have been used previously; try to avoid parking in the middle of some pristine meadow. Most good sites are likely to have had previous campers, and you will often find fire rings waiting for your marshmallows.

I could write for many pages about various boondock locations that we have enjoyed. However, I think finding them is part of the adventure. But I will share some brief comments about a few areas that we particularly liked.

Idaho's Stanley Basin and Sawtooth Valley – Boondocking and dry camping sites abound in gorgeous settings.

Southern Sierras – Lake Isabella and the Kern River are very scenic, though the highways are a little steep and narrow.

Pike National Forest west of Colorado Springs – Lots of sites scattered among the pines, with Pike's Peak dominating the skyline.

Wyoming's Wind River Range – Especially along the crystalline headwaters of the Green River.

Chama Canyon in New Mexico – Within a little known National Wilderness among multi-hued mountains.

Quartzsite, Arizona – Boondocking Mecca with vast designated and open camping areas in the desert.

As a parting shot, I offer the following photo, taken at Togwatee Pass off US 26 in Wyoming, along the Continental Divide.

A boondock toast: Here's to your fifth wheel happiness and success.

Appendix

With so many things to remember, especially when preparing a fifth wheel trailer for the road, many owners find that a checklist is a helpful device for ensuring that an important detail is not forgotten.

In this book we provide three checklists: Departure, Arrival and Setup, and Maintenance. Many of the tasks listed have been covered elsewhere in this book, but for the few not previously discussed, we have included a few notes below.

You may wish to photocopy these checklists. Or you can download printable copies at this web page: http://www.fifthwheelbible.com/checklists/. Have them laminated so you can use an erasable marker to check off the actions as they are completed. Place them on a clipboard and make a practice of reviewing them as needed.

Notes

Propane valves – Many RVers travel with their propane valves open so that they can operate their refrigerators on LP in transit. The RVIA recommendation is to close propane valves to reduce the possibility of a severe fire or explosion in case of an accident. It is always recommended that no propane appliance be in use when refueling the tow vehicle or refilling propane cylinders.

Refrigerator settings – For short trips your refrigerator can be turned off. It will stay cold several hours as long as it is not opened frequently. If your refrigerator has a 12 volt setting, use that during transit. On arrival use the automatic setting if you are hooked up to AC power. If you are dry camping, switch the refrigerator to LP to avoid draining your batteries.

Inverter – If you have an inverter for producing AC power, make sure that it is turned off in transit to conserve battery power.

Slideouts – Some slide mechanisms include a safety pin or other means of securing the slide in transit. Check your owner's manual and follow the recommended steps before taking your unit on the road.

Maintenance intervals – Rather than provide generally recommended maintenance intervals, we have simply provided a column on the Maintenance Checklist for you to enter either dates or mileages when various recommended services are due, based on your unit and owner's manual. Use the last column to record actual services completed.

Fifth Wheel Departure Checklist

Inside the trailer	
Loose items stowed	
Drawers closed & latched	
Cabinet doors secured	
TV antenna lowered	
Furniture secured	
Shower door secured	
Vent covers closed	
Windows closed	
Refrigerator door secured	
Refrigerator set on 12 v or auto	
Water heater off	
Furnace and/or AC off	
Water pump off	
Inverter off	
Slides retracted and secured	
Outside the trailer	
Door secured and locked	
Hand rail secured	
Steps raised and stowed	
Stabilizer jacks retracted	
Awning(s) retracted and secured	
Hookups disconnected, hoses and cords stowed	
Storage compartments secured and locked	
Propane valves closed	
Hitching procedure	
Adjust king pin height, extend or retract landing gear	
Lower tailgate	
Back and hitch	
Secure locking latch, lock	
Attach breakaway cable & plug in pigtail	
Hitch test	
Raise tailgate	
Retract landing gear	
Remove chocks & leveling blocks, stow	
Extend towing mirrors	

Fifth Wheel Arrival and Setup Checklist

Item	✓
Leveling and unhitching procedure	
Level trailer side-to-side	
Chock wheels	
Check level front-to-back	
Partially extend landing gear if trailer is high in front	
Lower tailgate	
Extend landing gear, use blocks as needed	
Detach breakaway cable & unplug pigtail	
Release hitch	
Drive truck forward	
Extend or retract landing gear to level front-to-back	
Outside the trailer	
Stabilizer jacks extended and firmed	
Hand rail and steps lowered	
Propane valves opened	
Hookups in place	
Awning(s) extended	
Inside the trailer	
Slides extended	
Vents and windows opened	
Refrigerator set on LP or auto	
Water heater on	
Furnace and/or AC on	
Water pump on	
Inverter on	
TV antenna raised	

Fifth Wheel Maintenance Checklist

Service Description	Service Due	Service Completed
Brake check/adjustment		
Brake pad replacement		
Wheel bearing repack		
Tire inspection and pressure check		
Tighten wheel lugnuts		
Battery inspection/service		
Lubricate hitch		
Lubricate slideout mechanical parts		
Condition slideout seals		
Roof inspection and cleaning		

About the Author

The author's first cross country RV adventure was in 1973. He's always had itchy feet and adopted the RV lifestyle full time in 2004, traveling with his canine buddy Timmy. He began writing for RV travel web publications in 2005. He is an avid photographer, hiker, fly fisher and sometime rockhound.

Made in the USA
San Bernardino, CA
24 November 2015